From the Field:

What Pastors Have to Say About Children's Ministry

A Report by
Constance Dever

THE PRAISE FACTORY
manufacturers of active minds, noisy joy, and prayerful hearts since 1997

Curriculum for preschool and elementary age children,
training tools, music and other resources
are available for download or to order at:
www.praisefactory.org

© 2022 Praise Factory Media

Scripture quotations marked (NIV) are taken from the Holy Bible,
New International Version®, NIV®. Copyright © 1973, 1978, 1984 by
Biblica, Inc.™ Used by permission of Zondervan. All rights reserved worldwide.www.zondervan.com

Scripture quotations marked (ESV) are from The Holy Bible, English
Standard Version® (ESV®), copyright © 2001 by Crossway,
a publishing ministry of Good News Publishers. Used by permission. All rights reserved.

Scripture quotations marked HCSB are taken from the
Holman Christian Standard Bible®, Copyright © 1999, 2000, 2002, 2003, 2009
by Holman Bible Publishers. Used by permission. Holman Christian Standard Bible®,
Holman CSB®, and HCSB® are federally registered trademarks of Holman Bible Publishers.

TABLE OF CONTENTS

Preface	5
Introduction	7

PART I Church-Shaped Children's Ministry In Various Church Settings — 9

Church Plants	11
Church Plants in Missions Settings	17
Church Revitalizations and Healthy Churches	21

PART II Comments from Pastors — 33

Straight from the Horse's Mouth	34
Leadership and Volunteer Position	35
Equipping Parents and Children through the Church Worship Gathering	41
Who's in the Worship Service?	45
Curriculum	47
Child Protection Policy	49
Recruiting Volunteers	51
Teacher Service Limits	53
Teacher Training	55
Teaching Teachers about the Gospel, Conversion and Discipleship	57
Baptism and Children	59
Parents Training Up Their Children	67
Coffee Shop Pep Talks	75
Snap Your Fingers	85

PART III Appendices — 87

Appendix A Elders' Position: The Baptism of Children at Capitol Hill Baptist Church	89
Appendix B Children's Church and Family-Integrated Church Models	93
Appendix C Children's Ministry: Past and Present	97
Appendix D Church-Shaped Children's Ministry: Mindful of the Gatherings	137
Appendix E Church-Shaped Children's Ministry: A Whole Church Affair	159
Appendix F Capitol Hill Baptist Church: One Example of Church-Shaped Children's Ministry	183

Preface

A children's ministry book for pastors written by a woman? What's that about!? Well, in case you were wondering what Mark Dever's wife has been up to (besides supporting him as wife and as mother to his children), here it is! All these years, as Mark has been pastoring here at CHBC and writing and speaking to other pastors about building healthy churches, some of it has rubbed off on me and my life's labor for the gospel among children, at home, in our community and in our church. Thanks to the leadership of Mark and the other pastors/elders, those of us deeply involved in children's ministry have had the immense blessing of being led by them in vision and in practice. They have cared well for families, yet not burned out volunteers. They have helped us to be the hands and feet of their God-given vision; and to understand our role as equipper and supporter, not usurper, of parents with their children. And, they have helped us to see that our goal is not just to help leave a legacy of truth in heads and hearts, but to prepare children to gather meaningfully in worship with the local body of Christ. After all, they are tomorrow's church in our midst today. We have come to call this godly, careful shepherding "Church-Shaped Children's Ministry."

Three times a year we share these ideas with pastors who come from around the world to a 9Marks Weekender here at CHBC. About halfway through this four-day, drink-out-of-a-fire-hydrant, crazy event, we lure as many attendees as we can into our stereotypically drab, old church fellowship hall with the promise of a free lunch. These men may be thinking food, but we hope to put a healthy serving of Church-shaped Children's Ministry on their pastoral plates. The men certainly seem to leave the lunch with their heads as full of encouragement and new ideas as their stomachs are with food-- maybe fuller. This little book is an attempt to share with you what we share with them at those Saturday lunches. And if you get to the end of this book and are looking for more, think about coming to join us. We would love to have you.

But until then, go grab your own lunch (sorry, we couldn't figure out a way to include a sandwich with this book) and start reading. Think of me as not so much author as scribe, describing to you what we've learned here at CHBC under our elders' leadership. And I, on behalf of our children's ministry team, hope and pray that you will be both encouraged and challenged by Church-Shaped Children's Ministry.

Constance Dever
April 10, 2022
Washington, D.C.

Introduction

The follow information I gleaned during interviews I conducted in the spring of 2020 from men who have gone out from CHBC to pastor churches around the world. They all have in common a 9Marks-of-a-Healthy-Church approach to pastoring that they have sought to apply to their particular church situation. Their decades of experience pastoring churches and thinking about serving families is summarized in this section. I was greatly encouraged at the consistent patterns of wisdom and good fruit that appeared in compiling their accounts.

"Preach and pray. Love and stay" is the simple model my husband gives pastors looking for their churches to become healthy or stay healthy churches. (https://www.9marks.org/article/the-priority-of-patience-prayer-and-preaching-in-church-planting/ is just one article that discusses these ideas. The 9marks.org website is filled with many other helpful resources like this!) Everything I've gathered from the pastors I interviewed points to the wisdom of this advice, even as concerns children's ministry. So grateful to all the men who took time to provide their thoughts! I hope you will benefit from their prudent counsel and experiences in the school of hard knocks.

I am presenting the pastors' feedback in two ways: first, by basic, church-type (Church Plant, Church Plants Overseas, and Church Re-vitalizations/Healthy Churches); then, by topic. The church-type overviews allow you to look at what pastors in a similar situation to you are thinking and facing. The topical comments give you a more complete look at what pastors are thinking and facing, regardless of their church type. I would suggest you read all the church-types, even if it's not yours. There is much to learn in what others are facing and you may face one day.

The appendices are filled with lots of materials to give you more depth of understanding and breadth of ideas. There are actually more pages in the appendices than in the main body of this report! But I decided that they would be more helpful for you than if I left them out. Make sure you look through them!

May all of these resources encourage you as you seek to faithfully serve the Lord and the families He puts under your care. Thank you for serving us!

Soli Deo Gloria
Constance Dever

Part I
Children's Ministry in Various Church Settings

What Church Planting Pastors Say about Children's Ministry

Transition Is Tough
Church plants frequently begin with a perfect storm of a few families, a lot of kids, rented, non-church facilities. Sometimes, only the pastors' family makes up the entire children's ministry, making in feel like an imposition to ask those without children to provide child care for the pastor's family. Even those with a larger number of charter members have difficulties. Frequently the adult members bring with them an equally large number of children. All may plan for what they think they will need or will and encounter, but they face weeks, even months of experimenting to find the best way to support their families in this new setting. On top of that, most church plants are sent out from a larger, established church where family life and children's ministry were more easily and more fully served. As much as you THINK you know that things will be different, you still have to experience it and that can be frustrating and discouraging.

Best Advice from Church Planters:

1. It's of Far Greater Consequence that You Might First Think
Children's ministry affects most of your church in one way or the other: your kids, your parents, your member volunteers, your happiness in your facility, your attractiveness to new families. And, since church plants are planted to grow, you aren't even just looking at how to serve your current families, you are thinking about how you will be able to soon serve many others.

2. Child Protection Policy (CPP) Comes First
If you intend, as you probably do, to offer classes or nursery care to families in your church, then you need a child protection policy. Get this in place first, even before you figure out what you will offer. Why? Because the child protection policy will help set safe boundaries on your plans for children's ministry. It will help you see the pros and cons and even "deal breakers" for having a nursery in a particular space or classes in another. A child protection policy protects children, their teachers, and really, your whole church. Child abuse not only scars children, it shuts down churches. Church plants are especially attractive targets to predators because they are often disorganized. This leaves the opportunity for abuse. Every state has its own set of particular policies. One of the best sources of help for you as you are setting up a CPP is a mega church in your state. This is because mega-churches have to get safety right. There are so many people involved. Obviously, you will take their ideas and then fit them to your much smaller situation, but at least you know what is important. Books like Deepak Reju's book "On Guard" can be helpful. Online services like "Ministry Safe" can be helpful in setting up training of workers and free up your very limited numbers of volunteer and staff.

3. Formal from the Start
It might feel kind of silly to have a formal CPP in place. And in some ways, just because you know each other so well, it might not seem necessary from that point. But the pastors I spoke with all said that one of the other reasons for having a CPP in place from the beginning, even if it seems sort of like play acting with a level of security that you don't really know because of your familiarity, is that it can get very difficult later on to add in the CPP when you start getting new member volunteers that nobody knows. Many pastors mentioned tsome of their charter members feeling insulted because suddenly they were being treated with a new level of security. They felt as if they were suddenly not trusted when the new, formal CPP was brought in. Better just to put in the formal CPP from the beginning and tell everybody

come in. Help your charter members get behind you and the safety of the kids before they need to think about it. Help them see how this is yet another way they are serving the gospel by submitting themselves to the CPP. And setting their church up for good growth in the future.

4. Plan before You Go
As you know your fellow church-plant pioneers, your families and facilities, you can begin to see what the needs of your starting church families are, what you might be able to provide, and where in your facility you might provide for those. Survey or interview your charter team members and see what their experience is and how much time they might be able to give to children's ministry. Cast the vision for children's ministry as an extremely important way to serve the ministry of the Word to parents among them, and future families who come. Sometimes those without children don't understand how very significant this is to their church plant. Tie it to the gospel, as it should be. Also explain that the elders won't just be thinking about the families' spiritual health, but the volunteers' spiritual well-being, too. This means that the elders will only choose to offer families what is within limits that serve all. But, of course, the more who are willing to serve, the more the church can offer before they reach those limits. Willingness to serve in children's ministry is something to talk about with every charter member.

Find out how many children you have in each age group. Talk to your parents about what they would most like to have. All of these things will help you see your children's ministry "budget" and where it would be best to spend it. Make sure parents understand that this is a wish list that will help the elders to form a vision and a plan. This is also a good time to share with parents that offerings will be (typically) much less than they are used to. One pastor told me that 150 members is usually the threshold for a sustainable, full-ish children's ministry program. That may be a number nowhere close to where your charter membership stands. Patience and sacrifice will be needed.

5. Get Advice
Speak to other pastors who have church planted about how they planned for children's ministry. These interviews with pastors showed me how much great advice there is and how many problems you can avoid by others' experiences. If nothing else, the 9Marks network will list many church plants that you could contact for input. This may be one of your wisest moves.

6. Plan before You Need
Even after you have started meeting and made your initial plans for children's ministry, you will need to plan for what's next. As mentioned already, the very nature of a church plant is to grow. Growth inevitably brings new families and more children, whether through births among current members, or through visiting families. And even where there is not growth in member numbers, children are growing. And as children grow, the needs and the potential opportunities grow. So, even if at first you only have a few families with a few babies, and maybe a toddler or two, think ahead to what is around the corner.

Try to build a flexible children's ministry that allows you to accommodate that family with a 2nd grader who shows up, even though you only have preschoolers, and so forth. There are a number of curriculums and resources that can stretch to be used in a multi-age setting. Praise Factory, New City Catechism, and Truth 78 are three that can be stretched. Praise Factory curriculum even has a Bits and Pieces section for every Bible Truth in which you can download just what you need: such as a story, a game and a take home/coloring sheet. All three curriculum are created to stretch and reach a 4-6-year age span (Hide 'n' Seek Kids, preschoolers; Deep Down Detectives, preschool to early elementary; Praise Factory Investigators, K-5th grade). Some churches have even used the curriculum with adults because it presents theological concepts that are deep enough for adults, but simple enough for kids. New City Catechism would also be helpful like this, too. Very simple app.

But even something as simple as a solid Bible storybook that you add questions to that might reach younger children as well as older children is a possibility. If you have more money than teachers with this ability, then you might lean towards a curriculum that does this. If you have more teacher power than budget, you might choose something more basic and have them write in the questions to create your own curriculum as you go. Praise Factory offers a lot of games for preschoolers and elementary school age kids that can be used with any Bible verse or Bible story. You buy the simple props and put them in a container, and you are ready for any of the games. Every game uses a set of questions. These are ready-made in the curriculum. But, you can come up with your own questions and apply them to your lesson. The games are available for download through praisefactory.org in the resources section. They can be super helpful to add to a simple lesson to add reinforce while having fun. And, can mean you are ready with something that new, older child might enjoy, while still being accessible to the younger children.

7. The Nine Marks Matter, Even in Children's Ministry
Over and over the pastors I interviewed gave examples of how their view of the church made a difference in children's ministry.

Elders Lead the Way
While you most definitely want to seek out the advice of other churches and the advice of members, families, gifted teachers within your church plant, you do NOT want them to take the lead. Elders need to lead the way. This was one of the most important points underscored over and over in the interviews. First, because pastors/elders are the overseers of all teaching. Children's ministry is an outflow of the responsibility God has given them. Secondly, because so much of your membership will be involved in children's ministry and the pastors need to care for the needs of all. They are in the best position to do that. Thirdly, because any changes or any issues that occur in children's ministry needs to be seen not as the work of those who carry out the vision, but of those who made the vision: the elders. And fourthly, because this puts everyone in children's ministry under the care and authority of the elders/pastors. And fifthly, because where the gospel is preached, God is at work. Conversion comes. And with conversion, comes discipleship, baptism, and membership. Pastors need to be the ones who decide how best to present the gospel to the children, and what the track of discipleship into membership looks like for children. This will be one of the thorniest issues, perhaps especially in America, that you will deal with, as the many pastors I spoke to can attest.

Expositional Preaching
Elders who preach expositionally feed and equip their church, their parents, for what God calls them to do. They might have little programmed children's ministry, but they know they are equipping the parents to be primary spiritual caregivers of their children. This is basic, biblical children's ministry. Knowing that the gathering is the main thing helped these men prioritize what kind of support programs they might offer and when to offer them. Such as, choosing to start with simple, child-care for parents with infants and toddlers so their parents can take part in the service, begins to make the most sense. Addressing children in the sermon or at least preaching from a simple outline made the sermon more accessible to them. Also, choosing to add a basic worship bulletin for preschoolers/elementary school age kids in the service is thinking of them, using the gathering, and keeping within the budget of very few volunteers at the outset. It will help you think through limits on serving during the service because you know your goal is for all to get as much as they can from the preaching. These are a few examples.

Gospel, Evangelism, Conversion, Discipleship, Membership, Church Discipline
These six all go together. They are the path from hearing the good news of Jesus to becoming a member. Usually, the children attending your church will be the majority of the non-Christians in your gathering on any given Sunday. As they are converted—or, as they or their parents think they are converted—

authority to elders, if their child is a minor and seeks membership, is huge!!! One pastor I spoke to lost a significant number of members over the "watch and wait" approach to baptism/Lord's Supper/membership The pastors I interviewed said to make sure this topic is broached with prospective members to avoid such problems. In the classroom, it is so important for teachers to understand how the conversion of a child needs more time to bear mature fruit and to be careful how they word the gospel.

Sound Doctrine
Pastors overseeing the approval of curriculum and teachers have a powerful impact upon the teaching of sound doctrine to children. If you don't take this lead, someone else will. And if you let someone else do it without your input, and they choose poorly, not only do you affect your children, but you are left with only a "reactive" response to the person who choose it. Far better to choose and develop regular feedback that guides and develops these well-meaning people. Keep them on your team and keep them fulfilling their desire to serve the church and the children.

8. Deacons Who Serve
In interview after interview, deacons were the godly, unsung heroes of children's ministry. They had a level of godliness that showed itself in servant-like humility to carry out the pastors' vision for children's ministry. They exhibited a selfless love to serve the families of the church in tasks such as cleaning toys, setting up and prepping resources, recruiting volunteers, helping teachers have what they need to teach, and greeting and signing in families/children in a way that is welcoming and protects their safety. And frequently, their sound doctrine helps answer basic questions, train others, and to know when to speak to the elders about any concerns they notice among the teachers. Many church planters said that these deacons/deaconesses were key to their children's ministry. They also said that if you can have multiple deacons/deaconesses from the beginning and split the responsibilities among them that it will help them not burn out. And, make sure to have term limits for these servant-hearted men and women! Really, you want to be looking for their replacement to train and to mentor as soon as they take the job.

9. Give Clear Expectations Over and Over
I mentioned giving clear expectations for the mereness of children's ministry to your charter members from before you even launch. You will do well to continue to remind your members of this as you go. It's one thing to acknowledge this before you start; or even to endure eagerly and bravely the first few months of much less children's ministry that you had previously, but it can get wearisome as time goes on. You may need to remind yourself of this, too, as you feel the pressure to add more programs when you don't really have the sustainable volunteers to do it. If you have your teaching priorities ordered and your volunteer limits agreed upon within your elder board, this can help you vision cast these to the congregation again and again. Make them a point of prayer. Ask God to bring you more teachers to grow to the next item on your teaching wish list. Explain to members it is an act of care for all when you tell them why such and such program can't be added yet. Of course, always be open to change and advice. We do learn as we go on.

10. Start Small, Start Slow, Wait for Sustainable
Every pastor I spoke to gave this advice. The concern that a new family will come, and you don't have what they want for their kids is a very common and real scenario. That's why you need to think very strategically about what is best to offer, since you usually can't offer everything from the beginning. That's also why it's good to choose a teaching program/curriculum that has that flexibility mentioned earlier., but also that you trust God! Care for whom you have! He knows your limits. He will provide. Some men even said that when they explained to the new families why they didn't have more (to care well for the whole membership) that was an attractive witness to them. It showed them good shepherding. Every church I interviewed had families come like that. Some did not stay. But every church has seen growth, nonetheless. You might wish you could have those families, but you do not want them if what

you have will lead them to frustration over and over.

It is a wonderful thing to be able to add in a program that serves more families. How nice to be able to say to visitors, "Yes, we have Sunday School to offer your children." But do not leap ahead and begin a program until you have sustainable volunteers for it. And not just sustainable for the upcoming month, but actually sustainable for six months or better yet, a year. And when you add, tell your congregation what you are doing. Such as, "We have sustainable volunteers for a year of Sunday School for these ages. We will launch this program on January 1 and will run it for a year, then re-assess. Please join us in praying and in participating in this new program."

11. Use the Worship Gathering as Much as You Can
The main point is the gathering. In the beginning, it may be about all you have, in terms of equipping families. Make the most of it. Assess your space. Is there a place where you can put nursing moms where they can hear but have a bit of privacy, such as in the back of the room? Is there an area where you can have parents with babies or toddlers, so their extra noise doesn't distract so many? Can you make the upcoming sermon Bible passage available for parents to read and discuss with their children ahead of time, so they can all learn more from the preaching? Can you make the songs you regularly sing available for families to use with their children? Can you provide some kind of worship bulletin? Can you preach using simple points, simple illustrations that kids can understand, or applications to their lives? These are examples of ways you can use the gathering to equip parents and teach children, too. Not only do you want to make the most of the gathering because it's children's ministry that every church can do, but also because the gathering is where you want all to be. Even when you are established and have the luxury of any children's ministry program you desire, it still all needs to point to gathering everyone together to worship. It just can't hurt to make the most of the main thing!

12. Don't Ask Your Wife to Be in Charge of Children's Ministry (if at all possible)
Church-planting husband, it may be very tempting to ask your talented (or at least willing) wife to be in charge of children's ministry. Please do not make this mistake! Your family will be under enough pressure just supporting you in this new venture. You will need her to be a big part of that. No doubt if you have kids, your wife will be taking her turn serving with the children. But do NOT put her in charge. If she is gifted in thinking about children's ministry things, she could even be a helpful support to you and to those who are shaping the program.... but do NOT put her in charge!!!

Children's ministry, especially in church plants, is fully of neediness and sometimes grumbly people. Shield her from that. It will be enough to have her wise input as you sort through those people and issues. Better to launch later than to put her in that position.

13. Avoiding Burnout: Places Where You Visit, Places Where You Live
There is no doubt that a church plant is all about "all hands on deck." You will need everyone you have to be completely invested. In the early days especially, people may serve more frequently in children's ministry than they will a few years down the road when your church has (Lord willing) grown. But asking people to give so sacrificially should be a place where you "visit." In other words, for a time as you are getting started at the beginning. Or, at a time when you have just added a new, additional program. It's ok to see those as times of increased expenditure of effort. But those are not places where you live. Not places where you keep asking people to serve because it will turn into burnout. A church plant is a maiden voyage. You plan the best you can. Do not feel bad if you must reassess when one of those "places you thought you would only have to visit" turns into a "place where you live." More important to care for all well than to die on the hill of a children's ministry program that is too big.

14. Adding Something New? Find Some Load Bearers First
When you start a new program, find a few members who are willing to own it and put in the sacrificial hours needed to get it started. This will be getting to know the curriculum and training volunteers. It will be breaking the typical service limits for a while as they are on hand to help others more than usual. As the program gets established and kinks worked out, then the load bearers work can move down to regular limits and simply glean feedback from teachers after class.

15. Youth and Youth Groups When You Have Hardly Any Youth
Youth groups are usually programs that come into their own as your congregation ages. Baby spring up and nursery care with them. But youth groups, most churches mature into them. A number of pastors told me how hard it was for their teenagers who had no youth group to be part of their church. Or, how at times they were frustrated when a family decided to leave to go to another church that had a youth group for their teen when the church plant didn't have anything. A number of pastors said that they were judgmental in their attitude and frustrated at the time. But, as their children became teenagers and still, they didn't have a youth group at their church plant, they became more understanding. They could see how very helpful that extra support from godly youth group leaders can be as a another helpful, mentoring voice in their children's lives. And the huge blessing it was to have events that didn't look just like the world and didn't require sex or drugs or some other kind of sinful behavior. A place where kids who felt the tug of the world and wanted to say "no" could meet and enjoy like-minded company. These pastors said they found great value in finding a youth group at another, like-minded church where their kids could be a part. They encouraged pastors to be understanding as parents of teenagers find that the need for their youth takes them away from your church. In time Lord willing your church will grow and you will have a flourishing youth group shaped and fed by the gospel. Here in CHBC it took about 20 years to get there!

16. Unexpected Group for Youth
But, on the other hand, one pastor told me how even though their church had no youth group, they encouraged the youth to attend one of the regular, adult small groups. They were amazed at the wonderful fruit and new, unexpected friendships that resulted, particularly among one group of teenage girls who joined a women's small group. These girls were nurtured and encouraged by these older women and got to see godly examples of the Christian life in those decades ahead of them. The one pastor who told me about this said he was encouraged that the body can help strengthen each other even as regards youth. Do not underestimate the value of these kinds of groups or creative solutions. Isn't this just another beautiful picture of the body of Christ loving and learning from those different from themselves?

What Church Planting Pastors in Mission Settings Say

Church plants in mission settings face the same sort of issues as mentioned above in church plants in your home country, except that now you add a new cross-cultural element. Here are some of the additional observations pastors in this setting shared with me.

1. You Bring Something with You
Church planters who go overseas bring with them their own church experiences from their own culture. It's important to identify those and realize when they are cultural elements and when they are biblical elements. Recognizing them can help you focus on using the cultural elements of the new culture that you are reaching on which to build your biblical foundation in this new setting.

2. Hold a Church Service Even if It's Just for Your Family
In some cultures, it may take a long time, even years, before you see your first national believer. Don't wait for new believers to regularly gather together for worship as a church, even if it's just your family. Those worship times hopefully one day WILL be something that includes new believers from the culture you're living in; but until then, you still are called to care for whom you have, even if it's just you and your wife and your children, if you have them. For your and their sake, you need to be gathering together as a church. Hebrews 10:25 tells us not to neglect to gather together. In biblical times, there were often very small churches in their first days. They didn't wait to gather. Neither should you. And don't just have a Bible study. Have a worship service! Include prayer, songs, Bible reading, and preaching. Take the Lord's Supper. Preach the Bible, pray the Bible, sing the Bible, read the Bible, see the Bible. This is so important for your family or team families.

3. Be Wise about Who to Teach
Recognize the authority system within the culture you are trying to reach in order to make the best decisions about when and whom to baptize; and sometimes, when and whom to teach. Some of the pastors I spoke with who were serving among unreached people groups found that it was important to understand the impact of the head of an authority group to begin learning how to read the Bible and becoming a Christian would have upon those under their authority.

For instance, one pastor told me that they learned that the young people worked more quickly to learn how to read and even to put their trust in Christ. But, they also observed in that culture, to proceed with the young people without waiting for the older adults was actually a hindrance to the older adults learning God's Word and (Lord willing) coming to faith in Christ, themselves. These pastors learned to focus on the adults first and watched the young people quickly learn how to read alongside their parents/adults. But this way, the adults remained in their position of respect and this was beneficial for this whole culture in receiving the gospel.

The same pastor also shared that when the head of a family became a Christian in the culture where he was serving, it was almost like a second thought that everyone else in his family should be known as Christians, whether they had saving faith or not. So, when it came to deciding who should be baptized, they had to very carefully discern whether a family member truly had become a Christian or whether they were following the cultural norm and switching over to a new religion of their father.

4. The Children of First-Generation Christians

The pastors I spoke with said it was particularly difficult to help "first generation" believing parents know how to teach their children. This was because many times only one parent would become a believer. The believing parent and the missionaries had to balance the marital relationship with the biblical mandate to train up your children in the ways of the Lord. A lot depended upon how willing the other spouse was to allow their children to learn these new truths.

5. Older They Are, the Harder It Is

Related to this, the older the children were when their parents become Christians, the harder it was to teach their children the new way of life in Christ. The older we get, the more baggage we have. That baggage needs to be unpacked and replaced with training in gospel truth and living.

6. Parenting Gatherings

Even just basic parenting styles can need to change radically when parents become Christians. One pastor mentioned gathering together all the believers in the city or even region to talk about what Christian parenting looks like. This can be particularly helpful where there are small pockets of new believers scattered throughout the area in little churches. It was encouraging for these parents to meet each other and share their difficulties as well as their words of wisdom for each other.

7. Connecting Youth, Creating Christian Families

Some pastors helped link young adult believers across their city (and sometimes even across their region, so that they had a chance to meet other young, single Christians and find a believing spouse. Not only was this wonderful for these men and women, but it was also great for the church. Here were couples starting out fresh, working together to teach them how to train up their children because there was agreement within the marriage relationship.

8. Teaching Materials

Often there is very little curriculum available for use in the native language. Usually it will be one of the missionaries translating materials they have, or they write for use with these new believers. One pastor shared how he wrote his own catechism to use with new believing adults and kids, because of course, both parents and children were new to Bible truths. In this catechism, he included not just the standard questions and answers like we may think of in traditional catechisms, but cultural questions and answers as well. He did this because he wanted adults and children to remember what it looked like for a Christian to live out their faith in their culture. This is true of any culture to some extent, but cultures with little or no contact with Christianity especially need help learning what discipleship looks like in daily life. New believers can greatly benefit by learning simple questions and answers to help them in this new way of life practically.

9. Persecution

In countries where Christians are persecuted, this catechism included preparing adults and children for the reality of persecution and God's faithfulness even in the midst of most difficult times.

10. Missionary Kids

A number of pastors mentioned that ministry to their own children was some of the most difficult children's ministry they faced. Missionary kids often have a special set of needs that must be remembered and treated with care. These children take part in their parents' decision to leave their home country and live in another country for the sake of a gospel. They face many sacrifices like their parents, but not with the same set of tools of maturity and often, without the same faith that motivates their parents from the heart. Life as a missionary family usually involves a lot of transiency, and transiency translates as loss. Even when families go home on furlough to the States, no longer does that home culture feel like their culture. They are caught between two worlds.

Getting advice from older missionaries as to how they help their children deal with these challenges can be of great benefit. Also, having a State-side church that adopts these families as their own and welcomes them can provide more stability. One pastor also mentioned how very helpful it was for MK teenagers to have young, 20-something godly men and women come from home to help out for a few weeks, a month, or longer. These interactions provide these MK youth with an opportunity to see other godly young men and women living their lives out for Christ. In the typical, isolated, small church plant situation, these kinds of role models are often very few indeed.

11. Help with Children's Ministry from Home

A number of the pastors mentioned how helpful it was when someone skilled in building a children's ministry program and or teaching children came for a month, three months or even a year to take charge of implementing the pastors' vision for children's ministry. And sometimes, for pastors with very little experience in thinking about children's ministry, this involved actually teaching the pastors how they can care well for children through children's ministry. The men I spoke to said this outside help made all the difference in helping them set up a nourishing, sustainable structure for the children and built confidence in the people who would teach.

12. Child Protection Policy

Because many of these little churches meet in homes, storefronts, hotels, or other less-than-optimal locations, a child protection policy can be very hard to enforce. Most churches that I interviewed simply did the best they could, given the circumstances where they gathered, always hoping and looking forward to a better location that could provide them the children with better protection.

Some decided to only have women serve with the children in these less than optimal settings because men typically are more likely to be predators than women. It was a way to offset the risk.

Pastors mentioned how very awkward it was even having a child protection policy in the early days of a very small church because of the formal treatment of people who knew each other so well. Some were offended, feeling that the policy made it seem like they were already under suspicion of being a predator. This is another reason to have a CPP in place from the very beginning and to teach people that this is a service of the gospel that requires humility but will be for the good of all, even if it feels awkward at first.

13. Volunteers Being Well Fed

These little church plant can last for years and years before volunteer numbers can rise. Pastors must think very carefully about balancing the desire to have children's ministry available every worship service and making sure the volunteers are receiving the spiritual food that needs they need themselves. This might look like providing childcare only on certain Sundays. Or, providing less childcare for only your very youngest, most noisy, least attentive infants and toddlers, just so more people could be regularly fed in the service. having a Sunday school class for kids that wasn't during the Sunday service, would allow people to help teach the children, but without interfering with them being fed spiritually in the worship service, themselves.

What Pastors in Revitalized or Healthy Churches Say

Most Everyone Is a Revitalization at the Beginning
Every church that is not a church plant is, in one sense, a church revitalization when a new pastor takes his vows. There is hardly a pastor who does not find something he wants to change or sees for improvement. The big difference in a church re-vitalization and a healthy church is felt in how change is viewed (attitude of trust or distrust among the members) and what structures (church covenant, statement of faith and constitution, elders and deacons, appointed like-minded helper staff and volunteers) are in place for pastors to lead that change.

Spectrum of Health
The difference between a healthy church and a revitalized church is where a church is in the process. In some churches, there may be only the senior pastor who has a vision for a healthy church. Next, he often helps this vision spread to the rest of the church leaders. With time, the biblical-ness of these ideas becomes rooted in the congregation itself through the preaching of God's Word. Being a healthy church becomes a pastor-led ground swell that flows out to bless the whole membership and every area of the church's life. Once godly elders are in place and the church owns these ideas, it is much easier for those elders to make the changes that help the church become more healthy and stay that way. Healthiness in a church is something that comes slowly and must continue to be contended for. No "once and done" here. That's why it's helpful to talk about the healthy church and revitalized church together because really, the revitalized church is just a church a notch or two over on the healthy spectrum from a healthier one.

Patient Love
"He tends his flock like a shepherd: He gathers the lambs in his arms and carries them close to his heart; he gently leads those that have young." –Isaiah 40:11

The first days of a new pastor at any church are mainly spent getting to know the members and loving them well. As he understands them more, he can feed them better on God's Word and gain their confidence that his affections and his actions are for their good. As he sees what needs to be changed, he slowly but surely teaches the congregation and helps them understand what a biblically healthy church looks like and what it would look like for their church to adopt these truths. Ideally, these changes eventually take the form of a new/updated church constitution, statement of faith, and covenant. They hopefully include recognizing a plurality of elders to lead the church; establishing clear, biblical guidelines for membership that express what it means to be a Christian. how to live as a Christian, and the promises members make to help each other be built up in Christ.

It may even take years to get to the point of this kind of healthy structure in a church revitalization, the pastors I interviewed told me. They said they spent a long time living out leadership where they were, with their churches in the shape that they were in. Things began to change as the members grew in trust and confidence in their leadership and through their preaching. As the church saw them act in wise, godly, and thoughtful ways that were for the best of the flock, this helped them have open ears to hear the new ideas the pastors were introducing. Eventually, this did lead to a new constitution and covenant. these pastors said. "Your example is a visual aid for the good leadership you hope to be able to provide to an even larger extent through a new covenant and or constitution," one man told me. "Because of course, it's not getting to a signed document and running with it. It's that by the church signing that document, they think it's true. The structure, the document, are symbols of the unity of heart. And that's why when you bring the congregation.

to the point of being in agreement with you concerning the constitution and the covenant), you are in a stronger place for them to listen, accept and be on board to do things differently in children's ministry."

The pastors I spoke to said that the element of teaching to bring a congregation to a new place and leaving the best you can where they are now is an extremely delicate dance. The footsteps of this dance fall across the whole church and most definitely, and sometimes most problematically, they affect or need to affect children's ministry, for the good of the children and for the good of the whole church.

Here are fifteen, important words of wisdom from the pastors in church revitalization situations regarding children's ministry.

1. "Start by Taking a Children's Ministry Physical"

Find out as much as possible about what is going on. Here's the kind of questions the pastors were trying to answer, many times in-directly and gradually through conversation and observation. Or, directly and more immediately through meetings with those involved. **They all cautioned to use your head! Find out what you can by detective work and with love, not with an Inquistion squad of doom!**

Leadership:
- Who is providing oversight to Children's Ministry?
- Are they volunteer or paid?
- What leadership did the previous pastor give children's ministry?
- Do they have any oversight from the pastors? On what matters? How frequently?
- Does the CMD (Children's Ministry Director) have any assistants?
- Are there any deacons/deaconesses who help?
- Any other regular positions, such as hall monitors?

Philosophy and Vision:
- Who decides the philosophy of children's ministry?
- What is the philosophy?
- What is the understanding about childhood conversion and discipleship and membership?
- Does children's ministry see itself as carrying out the pastors' vision or their own vision?
- Is the emphasis on getting in as many participants as possible, on conversions, on teaching Bible truths, on safety, on equipping parents, etc.?
- Children's ministry seen as preparing children to gather with the congregation in worship?

Programs:
- What kind of programs are offered? When?
- Any programs that are in direct conflict with the gathering in the worship service?
- Are there any "alternate" church services offered for children and teens?
- Any special events, such as VBS, etc.?

Curriculum:
- What are they teaching?
- Who chooses curriculum?
- What do they look for in curriculum?
- Who chose what's in place now?
- What do they like or dislike about the curriculum?
- How sound is the curriculum?
- Does the curriculum have take-home sheet resources for parents?

Teachers:
- Who is teaching?
- Who recruits teachers?
- Are they regularly attending church?
- What is the teaching rotation schedule, if there is one?

Child Protection Policy:
- Is it in place? Is it enforced?
- Is it up to date?

Parents:
- Do parents know they are the primary spiritual caregivers for their children?
- Do many parents train their children in Bible truth at home?
- Do parents ever use catechisms?
- What are the trends in discipline among families?
- Are there any strongly held opinions within the congregation regards family and church, such as homeschoolers, family-integrated church, church's job to raise kids, baby dedications, young baptismal age, invitations, VBS conversions, etc.
- What is the typical family life during the week look like? What priority is placed on spending time together?
- Do parents regularly encourage one another informally in conversation? In classes? In small groups?
- Does the church provide any training to help parents?

Gospel/Conversion:
- What is the typical gospel presentation like in the classroom? Among parents? Does it include repentance and a sense of discipleship?
- Is there a dichotomy being Jesus being Savior and Jesus being Lord?
- Do you have teachers rewarding children with candy when they pray a prayer in class?
- When do parents expect their confessing child to be baptized? Immediately? After showing fruit? Teenager? Etc.?
- Do kids ever get baptized and included in the church at programs outside of the regular church service and membership process (such as on retreats or camps)?
- What is the process of children becoming baptized? Take Lord's Supper? Become members? Has the church practiced some sort of associate membership for children/youth who have been baptized?
- Do kids take the Lord's Supper if they have been baptized?
- Has the church practiced much "re-baptism"/"re-dedication"?

Kids in the Gathering:
- At what age do kids typically join the worship service?
- Do you provide any classes or child care during the service?
- Are there any additional places for noisier, wigglier kids and their parents to be in the service but not distract?
- By what age are all kids in the service?
- Do you provide any worship bulletins or in other resources to help parents with their children in the pews?

Resources on Hand:
- Do you have a library? What kinds of books are there? Sound, unsound? Parents? Kids?
- Do you have a bookstore? What kinds of books are there? Sound, unsound? Parents? Kids?

Facility:
- What shape are the facilities in?
- Are they safe for the kids?
- Are they adequate for current needs?
- Are they used by other programs, such as daycare or a school during the week? Does this cause any conflict? Are those other programs well-insured?

2. "What's the Heart of the Matter?"

Another very important step is understanding how and why what is being done started being done in the first place. "Why are these teachers doing that? What's the heart it's coming from and what's the misunderstanding it's coming from? And where is the theology possibly that it's coming from?"

Remember that chapter in church history? Remember the standard Sunday school movement and the revivals? Remember the curriculum that came out of that time? What some other reasons why teachers are doing what they're doing? It may be as simple as because that is what they were brought up on: that same decisionistic, light-on theology, version of conversion they imbibed from the curriculum they use.

Have attendance and baptism numbers have been so stressed in the past that the teachers are happy to do things that encourage children towards (what appears to be) making a decision? Or, have teachers just been very poorly led in knowing how to effectively share the gospel with children? I know kids like candy, and adults like to reward kids for doing a good thing, but perhaps no one ever taught them that this might actually be hurting a child's soul as well as bringing on a cavity.

It is so easy to see what someone is doing and assume that you understand why they're doing it. And often, there can be many different reasons why someone is doing something. By taking time to find out where what they're doing comes from will help you have a better gentler conversation and more effective conversation with the same people as you trying to teach them.

And remember that preaching can be a conversation you hold with your whole congregation. It may allow a teacher or parent to hear without feeling defensive. And, it may lead to the very one-on-one conversations you are hoping for. Many pastors said it was through the preaching of the Word generally that they laid the groundwork for these conversations to be effective when they spoke to individual teachers.

And pray. Do not underestimate the power of the Holy Spirit at work. If it is a very hard task to ask parents and children to wait to become members, it is also very hard for pastors to be asked to wait and be patient as the congregation comes to unity in understanding with them. There's plenty of waiting to go around for everyone. No wonder patience is one of the fruits of the Spirit.

These sort of questions answers to these are questions will help begin to paint a picture of what your families are doing, what their needs are, what the church is been doing to support the families, what you can be encouraged as being done already, and what you put on your wish list to be able to change an appropriate amount of time.

3. "Child Protection Policy: One Change that Can't Wait"

Most things will need to change slowly, but one thing needs to change immediately. The kids must be safe. The volunteers must be protected. Your church needs to be enforcing practicies in keeping with your state's requirements and insurance policy requirements for safe childcare.

Child protection policies that are a custom fit for your church take a while to create. Even so, as soon as you find out there is a childcare safety problem, there are basic guidelines that can be put in place immediately. From there, you can work your way to a custom child protection policy being written and implemented. Insist upon these changes. "Ministry Safe" is an organization that has online videos that churches can watch. Their training videos but they're also videos that inform about the importance of a child protection policy.

Get the current children's ministry leadership behind you on this issue as soon as possible. If they are skeptical, show them one of the Ministry Safe (or other child protection videos) that bring home the sobering need for a child protection policy. It can be very disturbing when you see the potential for child abuse inside your church. If you can find out the shape and the regularity of enforcement of the child protection policy at the church before you get there, and get the leadership on board, it may be something that can be changed even before you were in the pulpit preaching your first sermon. One pastor I spoke to underscored this. He said as much as he did not like a particular curriculum being used because the teaching was rather moralistic, he felt that could wait (and of course, he would be clearly preaching the gospel from the pulpit, which would help immediately), but he absolutely could not wait to keep the children safe. He had to press in on that matter immediately, no matter how hard it would be.

4. "How to Introduce the Idea of Change"

Many of the men I spoke to said that children's ministry was one of the most difficult areas to introduce and implement change. That's because churches typically have a lot of people who really care about children's ministry, and many times they've been doing it the exact same way for a lot of years. There's a real ownership of what they do. So, for you to come along and say they need to change what they're doing because suddenly it's not good enough or sound enough, can feel rather offensive. These pastors said it helped to remember the hearts of love that these workers have for the children. Many times these faithful servants were older women who have been teaching for years and giving their lives for the children, in the best way they knew how to. Remember this and make sure to show your appreciation for the love and for the gospel that they probably meant to be at the heart of what they've have been doing for years.

Another common problem encountered by these pastors was a Children's Ministry Director (CMD) who had been allowed to do whatever he/she wanted. One pastor told me the CMD said to him, "You run the church, we'll run children's ministry," when he asked questions about the children's programs. It makes it even harder when the person running children's ministry is a woman. There are not many places in the church where women are given such leadership roles as in children's ministry. It may be hard for some women to give up the exhilaration of autonomy. And how very hard it is for the male pastor to approach this woman and explain this isn't male vs. female power struggle. This is placing her work under the care of pastors who are responsible before God for all of the teaching in the church. I personally have witnessed this very difficult dynamic in churches we have attended. Here at CHBC, the pastors chose the title Children's Ministry Administrator, not Director, in order to clearly cast the role as a support role that listens to and carries out the godly vision for children's ministry. The elders are actually the Children's Ministry Directors.

4. "How to Introduce the Idea of Change"

Even if the conversations get difficult and children's ministry leaders or volunteers respond with anger or hurtful words, these pastors said to still remember that the motives of these people are usually full of love, even as their words are full of anger. And, that many times they feel like they are being replaced or usurped. As an older woman, myself, now, I can understand better than ever that scary feeling of becoming obsolete. If you can find a way to encourage these servants about the wonderful things they have done and their years of service and bring them alongside with the good things you're trying to do in this new way, the chances are a little higher that you will help them be part of the change.

5. "Focus on the Parents, Not the Structure as Change Agents"

These pastors also said that rather than focusing on changing the structure, to instead, focus on talking to parents and preaching to the congregation about the sorts of things you're hoping to fill the children. This helps them become convinced of the good you want to do and makes it easier to see change as the natural out-working of achieving that good. This brings the church along with you and makes new changes and structure and curriculum more of a groundswell event, rather than a top-down enforcement.

One pastor told me he knew of bad teaching going on in some of the kids' classes. He decided to preach truth from the pulpit that would counteract this teaching in the class. After a while, the parents recognized the teaching was bad. They actually went to him and asked him to please change what was going on in that class, so that their children can have a good teaching that is in keeping with his sound preaching. That is a perfect example of this idea/approach.

6. "Baptism, Lord's Supper, and Membership"

Perhaps nowhere do things in children's ministry get more difficult than when you are talking about conversion, baptism, the Lord's Supper, and membership. In many church revitalization situations, teachers and parents (and even previous pastors) do not think about tying baptism and Lord's Supper to membership and church discipline. Instead, they often tied baptism and the Lord's Supper to a profession of faith, which may or may not be conversion. So, if a young child "prays a prayer," they are pronounced converted. Soon afterward follows baptism without further questions. And with baptism comes taking the Lord's Supper. In these cases, membership is seen as a separate addition when a child reaches adulthood.

Unanimously, the pastors I spoke to agreed that children can be converted at an early age. But they also agreed that it is prudent, given the nature of children to be developmentally in process, to wait until they are at least in their teens to be considered for baptism. At this age, they are better able to understand what it means to live as a disciple of Jesus Christ. They felt this was more in keeping with the biblical model of making disciples. This saves baptism and taking the Lord's Supper for a point in life in which a person can clearly enunciate to the elders and to the congregation the story of their changed life. They have become known generally known among the church membership as a Christian, and are ready to submit themselves to the elders' leadership. These pastors felt it was important to also help parents realize that their children, as a baptized member of the church, would be under the authority of the elders and the discipline of the church primarily; under their parents' authority, only secondarily.

This approach of "patient waiting, watching and encouraging" is almost always new and difficult for families used to linking baptism with any profession of faith. Parents either think that you are saying that children are not converted, cannot be converted, or, at very least, you are being unbiblically, overly cautious by waiting. Sometimes, actually many times, the real issue may be the parents want a sign from the church that their child is really saved. Yes, perhaps parents know baptism does not save, but it sure does look like it must really be conversion if the pastor is baptizing their child.

One pastor I spoke to quoted some horrifying statistics from a 10-year period in Southern Baptist history a few decades ago which tracked the number the percentage of teenagers who left the church after having been baptized as children. 80% of those baptized had left! During this same period in the same churches, 33% of adult baptisms were actually re-baptisms because the adults decided they weren't really Christians when they were baptized as children. Assurance through early baptism helps no parent or child, and it certainly does nothing for the purity of the church either.

However, helping parents accept a new "watch, wait, and encourage" baptism-membership connection can be a slow process. What helped the most? Conversations with parents and teaching from the pulpit, the pastors told me. Most of them also said that they did not set a specific age for baptism, but they did set in place a clear (and slow) track to baptism, Lord's Supper, and membership that was clearly more appropriate for someone who was at least a teenager.

Almost all the pastors said that it was easy to bring the congregation along with them after establishing an elder board and that leadership coming to a baptism position they could agree upon. They all stressed how important it was to share these views on baptism in the prospective membership classes and again in the membership interviews, so that no one would not be surprised. Most every church lost prospective members as well as current members over this issue. One church even had to excommunicate a 17-year-old baptized member who subsequently did not live as a Christian and would not repent of his sin after repeated teaching and urgings.

7. "Be Careful about Baby Dedications"

Tied very closely with the early baptism mindset was baby dedications. Pastors told me that these need to be handled with at least as much sensitivity as child baptisms. Parents love to bring their babies in front of the church and have them dedicated to the Lord. Unfortunately, some parents put too much stock in this action in terms of the possibility of whether a child will become a Christian in the future or not. Or, they just love the ceremony baby brought up front and praying for him or her. And those who have relatives from a paedo-Baptist background may actually be confused when they see baptistic churches hold these dedications.

A number of pastors told me how they handled devaluing and diminishing baby dedications. They moved them from prominence in the Sunday morning service to a special evening service. They asked parents who wanted their babies dedicated to first come to a special meeting to prepare them for the dedication. In that special class, he taught them what a baby dedication is and is it not: it IS a time of prayer for you to train up your child in the nurture and admonition of the Lord. It IS a time for those present to pray and promise to help you do that. It is a chance to pray for your child's conversion, but it adds no special "value" to them besides that. These pastors told me that the teaching time was helpful for the parents and it certainly diminished the number of parents desiring to dedicate their child.

8. "Adding Volunteer Limits: How and Why"

It's not unusual for many revitalization churches to have people who have served for years and years and children's ministry. It's not unusual for these people to rarely or if ever go to church. Pastors care for teachers and nursery workers by making sure that they do not over-serve in a way that is detrimental to their own spiritual growth. A pattern of serving week after week after week and not attending the service is definitely a pattern that is detrimental to our volunteers' spiritual health. Limits placed on volunteers help make sure volunteers feed their own souls.

Some volunteers are relieved to embrace the finiteness of their terms of service with the kids. These are the ones who will go to church when given the chance. These are the ones who might quit teaching children's ministry because they get burnt out. And these are the ones that you want to keep teaching because they understand they need to be fed before they are in a position to feed others, even if the others are children.

But as I mentioned above, there are those others where service to the church in nursery or teaching is almost an excuse to avoid going to church and having their souls fed. These teachers are the ones that complain when you bring limits to their service. These are the ones who often leave the church because they can't serve as much as they want to; and, they show that they don't really have an interest in the church as a body or in growing in the world themselves. These are the teachers that you don't want to be teaching your children. They are not growing themselves and don't seem to want to put themselves in a position to grow. It brings to question whether they are converted themselves, sadly.

Putting limits of service in place often brings to light a teacher's desire for the Word and God's people. And, it provides you with a natural way to bring relief to those who seek it. And, it provides a natural way to remove from the classroom teachers who do not. It may be the very act they need that helps them reconsider the state of their heart in a way that may actually lead to their salvation.

9. Beefing Up a Child Protection Policy"

The pastors I interviewed said that most churches had some form of a CPP in place already when they came to the church. However, most said, especially in very small churches, that it either was not a very full-bodied CPP or not very well enforced. Everybody knew each other and they were sort of lax about it because of the familiarity. Many pastors said how difficult it was to begin to enforce the CPP more rigorously and conscientiously. Especially when beefing up a CPP meant enforcing couples not serving together alone in the same class. Over and over, that particular addition to a CPP, which is very necessary, was one that insulted volunteers. Again, it probably is better to start with a training video that shows the dangers of abuse, combined with a talk from the pastor sympathizing with the awkwardness of this change. You aren't making this change because you're suddenly suspicious of the volunteers who are helping now, but because when new volunteers come in whom you don't know, the church is set up to keep the children safe. Help them see again it's part of loving one another in a way that feels costly. The more that you can underscore that this is not because you suddenly became suspicious of them, the better chance it is of this being well received. A number of pastors said that they did lose husband and wife volunteers over the specific CPP policy. It's hard to lose anybody who will volunteer with children's ministry. And I have yet to meet a pastor who says, "We're good we don't need any more volunteers. And if anything, we're asking people to serve less." Most every church needs more volunteers. But just like every other part of the revitalize church, you have the previous pastor's church—the one that is there when you come. And bit by bit, you will have your church—the one that reflects your teaching, leadership and vision. There's going to be changes on the way and not everyone's going to like them as much as you would love for everyone to receive things and stay, if they can't receive things and cheerfully stay, then sadly you need to wish them well and let them go. It will be hard in the short term, but it will be better in the long term. You will look back on those days and you will be grateful for where you are with the team that you have who is uniform and unified and is keeping the kids safe.

10. "Bringing in New Curriculum"

Bringing a new curriculum is another place the children's ministry can ruffle a lot of feathers. Some pastors found it better to leave moralistic teaching in place a little bit longer than they would like (and preach clearly from the pulpit) in order to give the teachers time to be well-fed under good preaching, learn sound doctrine, and begin to see for themselves that the curriculum should be changed. Others found that as they added new classes, they could more easily introduce new curriculum into those classes. Then gradually as the older teachers retired, they filled those classes also with the new curriculum, too. Obviously, we want the best curriculum going into those little children as soon as possible. But it all goes back up to the point of balancing loving teachers tenderly and being patient, with getting everything optimal quickly. No two pastors approached the need for new curriculum the same way. And that goes to show how much nuance and knowledge of your congregation needs to go into how and when you change curriculum.

11. "The Difficulty and Importance of Youth Group"

As difficult as kids in children's ministry may be, many pastors who had church is large enough to have a youth group, found youth group almost issues perhaps even more difficult than the younger kids' issues. Youth group was difficult for a number of reasons.

Excitement to Keep Them Coming Back
Parents may force their little kids to go to Sunday school, but by the time those kids become teenagers, it becomes much more of a fight to get unwilling teens to go to church, let alone youth group. Teenagers can be much slower to do something just to please their parents. They are affected so much more by what their peers think or what they've come to value themselves. They are becoming their own persons fully.

It is extremely tempting in the world of youth ministry to make things exciting and fun like the world to get them to come to church. This is also why many churches have a separate youth church service tailored especially to youth culture. While we definitely want to scheme and use activities that youth like as vehicles for the gospel; but unfortunately, the gospel gets left out of the vehicle and youth never get to smell the aroma of Christ in a church service or in a simple Bible study. There is a lot of pressure on pastors to keep these events coming. And it's not the kids, but the worried parents of kids that are often those putting on the most pressure.

The pastors I spoke to said that having conversations with parents rather than taking an ax to these programs was the more effective way to both convey love, to convey the importance of the gospel, and to bring good changes. Gradually parents came to see the fruit from Bible studies that looked boring, actually produced a far deeper impact on their teens.

Hardest of all, the pastors told me, was making changes when there was an event-driving youth pastor in place. Until he can be on board or until he leaves it can be very difficult to see changes. But the process of getting him to leave was often very stormy.

"If they are not Christians by the time they are eighteen then they're probably not going to become a Christian." This is a very common quote even today in many churches in the South. This is another reason why parents get so desperate to do whatever is needed to get their kids to church. Again, teaching from the pulpit of God's ability to convert anyone and comforting parents with those truths is a slow but necessary way to contend with this life.

Youth Camps

"Decisionistic" youth camps are very popular. In these mountaintop experiences, some teenagers hear the gospel and truly are converted. Sometimes they are simply swept up in the emotion of the moment or in the actions of their peers. It is not usual for leaders at these camps o(r the youth pastors who take the kids to the camp) decide to immediately baptize all who have made a profession of faith, not seeing the importance of baptism being tied to membership or the need to give a confession time to bear fruit of repentance consistently life before someone is baptized—especially if that someone is a minor.

One pastor told me that he urged parents and camp staff not to do this, but if it were to be done, in order for it to "count" as part of the process towards membership, a video would need to be taken off the baptism, and the teenager would know that when he or she got back, he would need to go through membership classes, an interview with an elder, as well as give their testimony at church. He told me that these steps helped to limit these on-the-spot baptisms, and were a beginning down the road to them not happening at all.

12. "Pastors' Kids"

Nowhere is it more difficult to be a parent who wants to give their child or teenager time to make a true conversion of their own than with pastors' kids. Again, particularly in the South, where there's so much culture that says, "If you're Christian, your child should be a Christian," The pastors and their kids may understand why they are waiting, but there is so much pressure upon them and comments to have their kids show up as spiritual successes by being baptized. This takes a lot of prayer and a lot of support for your kids.

13. "New Wine for New Wineskins"

A number of pastors sent their children's ministry director to a like-minded children's ministry conference, such as the one Truth 78 puts on or that we put on here at CHBC. Sometimes going away and hearing from other people the same kind of things you're trying to convey can make the new vision you bring less personal. It can help them catch the vision for what you are trying to do and give them great practical help in understanding how to do it.

14. "New Wine for New Wineskins"

Looking for or bringing in new like-minded leaders or teachers to help put legs to your vision can be a huge help. Sometimes, you can bring the old leaders along by helping them catch the new vision. But sometimes it's just too big of a leap for them and they choose to retire. New leaders give you an opportunity to unify the vision and multiply your eyes of care for all of those who are serving or taking part in children's ministry.

15. "Burn-out Alert"

Many pastors said that Children's Ministry Directors often left of their own accord because of burnout. A Children's Ministry Director (CMA) that lasts more than a few years is a very rare bird. So, while you want to care well for your Children's Ministry Director, if even if you do, chances are they will be leaving soon. This is very hard when you have a good partnership. But, when that shared vision is missing, the open position will give you an opportunity to bring in somebody more like-minded. Make sure to treat your Children's Ministry Administrator well with regular meetings, talking not just about what is going on in children's ministry, but about how they are bearing up under the load. If you want to keep them longer, you need to provide them with more help, whether that be deacon/deaconesses, team leaders to take charge of different programs, or other volunteers/even paid assistants as you are able. And, always be on the lookout for someone to be mentored by your CMA, so that your CMA can have regular vacations while they are on staff; or, to be a possible replacement when the current CMA retires. Many pastors said they really had no idea how very taxing it was to oversee children's ministry and wished they had brought more assistants alongside their CMA sooner.

Comments from Pastors

Straight from the "Horse's Mouth"

In this section, I've grouped the background information that I used to describe the church settings in the previous section.

I certainly learned a lot by grouping everyone's comments by category, since you can begin to see patterns across every church type. I hope you find their responses helpful to you as you think through children's ministry in your pastoral setting.

Questions about Children's Ministry Leadership and Volunteer Positions

"How do pastors/elders lead children's ministry at your church?

- "They equip the congregation, including parents and children, through the preaching of God's Word."

- "They love the members under their care, including families, and pray for their well-being."

- "They desire to provide support for parents through children's ministry, yet protect the worship gathering, knowing it to be of primary importance. "

- "They encourage the church membership to help each another in raising the children in their midst through their words and their acts of service."

- "They provide pastor oversight of families, programs and children's ministry volunteers."

- "These men are called by God to be the vision-casters and shepherds of children's ministry, its doctrine and practices."

- "They lead by providing teaching priorities; approving program and curriculum choices, and, by setting healthy limits on volunteering."

- "They protect children of volunteers through a child protection policy."

- "They encourage, advise, support parents, teachers, and the children's ministry team."

- "They hold regular meetings with the children's ministry leaders to best care for all involved."

- "They care that the gospel is clearly preaching and that those who profess Christ as Savior are discipled."

- "They make decisions about the prudent age for baptism, partaking of the Lord's Supper and membership. They lead the membership classes and interview all who are considering membership. They speak with parents who have questions about the baptism of their children. "

"Do you have one elder/pastor who has special oversight of children's ministry?

- A few answered: "As sole pastor, I have that responsibility."

- Most answered: "An associate pastor is designated with special oversight."

- The larger churches with salaried CMA's preferred for oversight to be given by a staff elder/pastor with this responsibility because of the hours involved caring for the CMA and other duties.

LEADERSHIP AND VOLUNTEER POSITIONS

"What duties or responsibilities does the pastor/elder with special oversight of children's ministry have?"

- "He is responsible for keeping in regular contact with any children's ministry leaders and with knowing what was going on in the programs. Ideally, he meets with the children's ministry administrator in person or via email/phone every week."

- "He reports back to the rest of the elders with updates and bringing to their attention any issues that needed discussing more broadly."

- "He is directly involved with formulating and updating the Child Protection Policy."

- "He is the pastor/elder most directly involved in recommending deaconess and children's ministry leadership personnel."

- "He watches over the CMA and helps her avoid burn-out by asking questions about spiritual health, frequency in the services, and if she is working to create a children's ministry is not solely dependent upon her. He helps push her to build a deep-bench of CM leaders and volunteers, relieving dependence upon her."

- "He helps with any initial curriculum choices, program needs, and teacher changes."

- "Is the first pastor to deal with any concerns over curriculum that he either addresses himself or takes back to all the pastors/elders for their consideration."

- "He may help recruit volunteers, particularly men volunteers to serve in children's ministry."

- "He sometimes teach parenting or children's classes. He sometimes helps train teachers."

- "He is on hand to help with any difficult issues with parents, children and teachers."

- He has many of the conversations with parents concerning their children.

- "He sometimes faces being over-worked or neglecting children's ministry needs by not having enough paid or volunteer help to implement the regular needs of children's ministry; or, because he has been given other large concerns of the church to oversee as well. Give this man some deacons and deaconesses!"

"Do you have someone designated to carry out the pastors/elders vision practically? What do you call this position? What do they do?"

Most churches had underneath this pastor/elder, a Children's Ministry Administrator or Director. This person, sometimes a man, but often a woman, is directly responsible for the carrying out of the pastors'/elders' vision, including:

- screening and approving volunteers for service in children's ministry
- overseeing scheduling
- curriculum preparations
- keeping classrooms safe and clean
- coordinating training of volunteers
- communicating with the pastors/elders
- communicating with parents
- communicating with deacons/deaconesses and any other leaders/support volunteers

Sometimes this person is an unpaid volunteer. Many times, as the church budget allows, this is a paid, full-time or part-time staff person.

The elders at CHBC personally choose the title of Administrator over Director, helping the very title of the position be a reminder that this person's primary job is to carry out the vision of the elders, not to make elder-like decisions themselves.

LEADERSHIP AND VOLUNTEER POSITIONS

"Do you have deacons and/or deaconesses that help with Children's Ministry? What do they do? How long do they serve?"

- "They are recognized by the church to share the load of Children's Ministry, under the direction of the CMA."

- "Deacons/deaconesses are assigned a particular area of focus, such as training or recruiting volunteers, or prepping classrooms."

- "They are especially on hand on Sundays, aiding the needs of teachers, parents and children."

- "They usually supervise the signing in and out of children from any Children's Ministry classes."

- "These servants report back to the CMA any situations that need further attention, such as difficulties with children, teachers and parents, or more practical issues related to the classrooms, the child protection policy or classroom material needs."

- "They serve in ways that allow the CMA to be regularly in attendance in the worship service."

- "They rotate Sundays so that they are also regularly in attendance in the worship service."

- "Some members of churches being re-vitalized find the idea of "deaconess" very difficult for the church to understand. These churches usually have been using the title "deacon" to be used for non-pastor elders. And indeed, if deaconess was being used with that connotation, they would be correct to object. However, when elders are called elders, then that frees up the word "deacon" and "deaconess" to be understood in its biblical context. This is a position of service to the physical needs of the church under the leadership of the elders. Coming to this biblical understanding of deacon/deaconess can take a long time in such churches. Treat the members with patience, gentleness and clear, biblical teaching. And, while the title may not be used, pastors can still help the church recognize and appoint such men and women to the positions the title describes."

"Do you have special volunteers that help with Children's Ministry, yet do not have direct contact with the children? What do they do?"

- "We have some volunteers who do not spend time in classrooms with kids. They usually don't do their work on Sundays, but ahead of time, in preparation for Sundays."

- "They prep the classroom, such as cleaning toys or refilling supplies."

- "They prep the materials a teacher will use, such as photocopying or cutting out crafts."

- "They are support workers to the CMA or the deacon/deaconesses, helping to carry their load."

LEADERSHIP AND VOLUNTEER POSITIONS

"Do you use Hall Monitors and what do they do?"

- "Hall Monitors are (male) volunteers who patrol the childcare areas and public spaces in the church to ensure the physical safety of the children."

- "Hall Monitors may be called upon to help with child evacuation and emergency response to unauthorized persons in childcare areas. They often use walkie-talkies to keep in contact with teachers and the deacon/deaconesses on duty."

- "Hall Monitors often are called upon to make extra copies or get needed supplies during class time."

- "Hall Monitors assist teachers with getting the children to their classroom when there is a mid-service dismissal (such as programs that take place during only the sermon portion of the worship service."

- "Hall Monitors serve on a rotation so that no one regularly misses the worship service."

"What kinds of volunteer positions do you use in Children's Ministry?"

Team Captains/Coaches: Teachers who oversee the other teachers serving alongside them in a class or childcare. They help new teachers get acclimated and provide hands-on training.

Caregivers: Nursery workers (no curriculum) for children age 2 and below.

Sunday School Teachers: Teachers who teach in a time other than during the worship service, usually before the morning service.

Worship Service Teachers: Teachers who teach during part or all of the morning or evening worship service.

Class Assistants: Volunteers who serve alongside a teacher. They do not have teaching responsibility but are simply there to be an extra set of hands to help the teacher. These are usually middle school or high school students, children of members.

Questions about Equipping Parents and Children Directly through the Church Worship Service

"The basic, biblical model of Children's Ministry is equipping God's people through the worship gathering. How do you equip parents and children through your worship service?"

"We offer special worship bulletins."

These resources or elements were mentioned:

- Truth: 78 Worship Books

- Weekly, customized worship sheets based on the actual worship service.

- Points of the outline typed in.

- Made a sermon grid for the kids to fill in during the service.

- Words to listen for in the service/sermon.

- Favorite song and why.

- Plain paper with writing supplies. Kids asked to draw a picture of something from the service and give it to the pastor after the service. He put up the pictures in the church office each week.

- Basket with crayons and sermon note sheets

- Activity bag with worship sheet and writing supplies, not all items necessarily related to the service, but would keep the kids occupied.

- Provide children with a special notebook. Kids were told to go tell a (non-family) member something they learned in the service and got a sticker. When they accumulate 12 stickers, and they got a little prize. The idea is to help the children listen, AND, to make connections with other members in church at the same time.

- One worship bulletin for preschool-aged children and one for elementary/middle school kids.

EQUIPPING PARENTS AND CHILDREN THROUGH THE CHURCH WORSHIP GATHERING

"We equip through the songs."

These resources or elements were mentioned:

- "Encourage parents to take home the bulletins with the songs in them to teach at home to their kids."

- "Have links to mp3's of the songs on your church's website for them to access at home."

- "Introduce the songs during Sunday School to familiarize children with the words and the melody; even take time to explain words like 'grace'."

- "Worship leader takes time to explain the key meaning or a key Bible word (like "sin" or "grace" before the congregation sings a song to help kids connect."

- "Choose at least one song with simple melody and lyrics for children to easily learn."

- "Introduce, then repeat a song or two for a few weeks in a row so that parents and children have a chance to be familiar with it."

"We equip through the preaching."

- "Include application for children and parents in your sermon application grid."

- "Frame at least one illustration in a way that is accessible to children."

- "Use a simple, clear outline. Children will at least be able to follow that. Try to keep giving them the big picture of God's plan, and the gospel."

- "Aim for simple, relatable, robust preaching that all might hear and learn."

- "Sermon writing pitched at a sharp 16-year-old is a good level to feed most everyone something, even the youngest."

- "Regularly address the kids in the sermon: some said weekly, others monthly, others, whenever the text points to it."

- "Give the kids something to ask their parents after the worship service."

- "Address children at least once in every sermon, even have guest preachers do this."

- "Preach gospel clearly and simply every sermon, realizing that every service, the kids, if no one else, will be in need of responding to it themselves."

- "Try to engage the kids even if they don't look like they are listening. They usually are hearing more than you think."

- "Ask for kids' feedback during some point of the sermon."

- "Read resources like "Parenting in the Pew" (Robbie Castleman) and "Children and the Worship Service" (Sally Michaels, Truth 78). You can get wonderful ideas for how to help those parents with their children in your pews each week."

"Any other advice on how to equip parents and children through the worship service?"

- "It may seem hard to have younger children in service, but give them time and they learn."

- "The regulative principle (Sing the Bible, read the Bible, preach the Bible, see the Bible, pray the Bible) is multi-sensory in a way that can help kids learn."

- Small Church Planters: "No matter how small you are, be a church with your family. Start out as you intend to go."

- "Always address the 4-5-year-olds at the beginning of the service. Have them raise their hands to identify themselves at the beginning encourages them."

- "Acknowledge the children's presence in the service in some way each time."

- "The younger the children, the more careful you need to be about sensitive topics. This is an adverse effect on kids and makes things more difficult for parents. Tell parents ahead of time; or, set up an evening service address/Sunday school address, etc. where you talk about these things with kids not present."

- "Provide a "wiggly room" with video feed."

"Do you offer any programs to equip children other than through the worship gatherings? If so, what and when?"

In additional to child care (no teaching), many churches offered a few other programs, as volunteer numbers allowed.

- Sunday School was the number one program offered outside of the worship gathering.

- Youth group (usually on non-Sundays) was the second program most commonly offered.

- Some also had Sunday evening programs.

- Some had AWANAS, such as on a Wednesday night.

Who's in the Worship Services?

> **"Do you provide child-care or classes for children during the worship service?"**

All the pastors I spoke with understood the worship gathering to be the "main thing" that they wanted all members and their children to be a part of, eventually. They also understood that providing childcare and even some classes for children during all or part of the worship service was a very helpful support for equipping parents as well as preparing the children to gather. Here's who they included in their services and what they provided for those not in the services.

0-2 Year Olds

- Most churches provided childcare for this age group. They saw this as being the top priority for children's ministry: providing an opportunity for parents to be better equipped to turn around and train up their children. If they could provide only one thing it would be this.

- Some only provided for 6 months to 2 because so many parents kept their babies with them anyway; and, typically, these smallest infants are fairly sleepy and quiet still.

3 Year Olds

- Some provided childcare, some teaching for these children during the whole service.

- A few included 3-year olds in part or all of the service.

4 Year Olds

- Often at this age, churches chose to include children in the whole worship service, or at least up to the sermon before going to a special class of their own.

- Some provided childcare (no teaching for this age group, usually due to small childcare area that was suitable for just one group of 0-4-year-olds, making teaching not possible.

3-5 Year Old Preschoolers as a Group

- Some provided them teaching through the whole service. Some during the sermon only.

- Many grouped this age range together for teaching that did occur.

- Others split the 3 year olds off from the 4-5-year-olds.

5-8 Year Olds

- This group was fairly evenly split between having them in the whole service or in up to the sermon, providing them with teaching.

9 Year Old and Up

- This group was almost unanimously in the whole service.

UK Model: Ages 0-11's

- Sunday School held during sermon portion of the service.

- 0-2-year-old "creche" childcare usually provided for the entire service.

Making Changes to the "Stove-Pipe" Model

- Many pastors of larger, re-vitalized churches found that the children and even youth attended for their own, special, "whistles and bells" service, with no intention of bringing them into the main, worship gathering. This has been called a "stove pipe" children's ministry model by some: kids start in and grow up all the way and out of the church without ever being a part of the worship gathering.

- These extra services were extremely popular, and they had to act very slowly and carefully to correct this "stovepipe" mentality to worship.

- These pastors who encountered these programs all said that they have been slowly shaving off the maximum age for these services, gradually joining the youth/children into the service.
- They also worked to shape what happened during these services.

- Some also proclaimed 5th Sundays or summer or Christmas, etc. special Sundays where everyone would join together and there would be none of these "alternative" services held.

Curriculum

"What curriculum do you use?"

Most of the curriculum used by the churches I interviewed was created by churches that they knew and trusted. Gospel Project was the major exception to this, but its content was derived from pastors.

Formal Curriculum Used

- Children Desiring God/Truth 78
- Generations of Grace
- Gospel Project
- Grace to You curriculum
- Long Story Short, etc Machiowski
- Praise Factory
- Treasuring Christ
- Writing their own, in-house curriculum

Other Materials Adapted for Use as Curriculum

- New City Catechism
- Reading from a storybook Bible
- Inductive Bible Study
- Based off of their own church service worship bulletin

CURRICULUM

"What curriculum do choose and implement curriculum?"

Most of the pastors I spoke to followed a version of the following process:

- The elders chose a few curriculums that they were familiar with from previous use or by recommendation.

- They checked the curriculum for soundness, then usually passed it off to a knowledgeable team of members/ teachers for their opinion for what might work best at their church, given volunteer, space, budget, etc. constraints.

- The elders and curriculum team met together and came up with the best decision. Teachers were designated to begin to customize the curriculum to fit them.

- These teachers remained the "load bearers" who invested in teacher training and extra time in the classroom to help the adjustment.

- After a time, these load bearers would be in the classes less, and provide mainly feedback and incidental adjustments.

Child Protection Policies

Here is what the pastors said about how they developed, implemented and continue to update the child protection policy at their church.

"When did you create a Child Protection Policy?"

- **Church Plants:** before they had their first service. Most church planters could not underscore highly enough the importance of having this in place before they offered any childcare.

- **Overseas Family "House Churches":** as they added other families. First, more informal; then beefed up as they grew. (less than ideal).

- **Church Re-vitalizations:** All the pastors I interviewed said there was some sort of CCP in place when they became pastors. However, some were not very stringent or not very enforced. They said while other children's ministry changes could wait, this is the one that could not. Absolutely not.

"How did you create your Child Protection Policy?"

- "One of the elders took charge of the CPP and the background checks and application process."

- "Committee led by elder and including other members to draw it up initially. Then went to all the elders for their approval."

- "CPP's have special guidelines, state by state. Many reached out to mega-churches in their state for best examples and then adapted it."

- "Looked at Deepak Reju's book, On Guard, for ideas."

- "Got ideas from other churches of the same size and facility type as theirs."

"When do you update your Child Protection Policy?"

- "Update every 1-3 years as laws steadily change."

- "Regularly updated and re-visited as growth/building/etc. classes occurred. Every change requires a re-visit to assure you are keeping everyone safe."

"What is included in your volunteer approval and placement process?"

- "Must be a member 3-6 months before they can serve."

- "Application with references"

- "Background check. References checked."

- "Ministry Safe Online basic training videos that include a quiz."

- "Child Care Training Class offered during Sunday School hour or after church."

- "Interview with potential volunteers to decide where to put them."

- "Put them in a serving potential with other, more experienced volunteers to allow new volunteers to learn, and to provide a watchful eye on the new volunteers' interaction with the kids."

"What has been particular hard to enforce?"

- Start with formal guidelines in place as tempting (and unnecessary) it may feel to go with casual. It is very hard to go from "casual" to formal later because some members get offended, feeling like you are suddenly suspicious of their behavior. Tell the volunteers that it's good for visitors and to be ready as the church grows. Make it a service-oriented thing, not a "we don't trust you" thing. It may feel like "play acting" asking parents to officially sign their children in and out or for teachers to make sure to keep classroom policies, but it's for the gospel.

- Can be hard to enforce a CPP because some "cowboy" teachers either forget or choose Moving away from couples not serving on their own together. Many lost volunteers over this. some of the old volunteers because of this.

Recruiting Volunteers

"How do you recruit volunteers for Children's Ministry?"

Here are the various ways volunteers are being recruited in the churches I interviewed:

- **Pastors/Elders/Deacon of Children's Ministry Contacting Prospective Men Volunteers** It's true. There's often a lot more women serving in children's ministry than men. But men can have such a big impact on kids! Having the pastor/elders/or deacon of children's ministry speak to men helps to get other men to volunteer.

- **Member's Meetings** Many pastors recruit members for children's ministry during the children's ministry report in the members' meeting. This is a great time to let the congregation know what opportunities there are to serve as well as share fruit from what is happening already.

- **Announcements** Announcements at the beginning of a worship service for more children's ministry volunteers were common. Some churches even choose an especially eager member volunteer to stand up and share their experience and plug working with the kids.

- **Deaconess/CMA Speaking to Prospective Volunteers** Often is it one of these people who speak to new members about serving in children's ministry. Some larger churches used computer software that would automatically send an alert to the new member and the CMA about who has become eligible to ask. This is especially helpful for churches who have a waiting period. Easy to forget to see who can be newly recruited with so many other needs to be tended to.

- **Oversized Teams** Recruiting in "over-sized" teams that use volunteers on a rotation basis frees up teachers to not teach every week and this makes teaching more appealing.

- **Mentors** Offering skittish volunteers the opportunity to be an assistant under a more experienced teacher helps them grow in confidence in the classroom. It can make the difference between someone choosing to serve or not.

- **Separate Recruiter for Nursery and for Teaching Classes** Nursery and classes where teaching takes place uses two different kinds of volunteers. Having a separate recruiter for each group helps lighten the load and protects from burnout.

- **"Class Closed" Signs** CPP and insurance companies place limits on child-to-teacher ratios. If a classroom exceeds these limits, then it must be shut to additional children. Unless another teacher is willing to step in for that particular Sunday or join the class teaching team. Some churches put a notice on the door that shuts the class, but provide a number to call/place to go to offer to be an additional teacher to the class. The class can then be given approval to open and receive more kids until the new allowable number of children is reached. The outcome of these closures often results in more volunteers.

- **Display board code during service** Some churches have display boards that are used not just to alert parents that their child needs them (each family has a number), but also to display codes (ours is 100) which means we need last-minute help.

- **"We will shut down" Warnings** Sometimes there is an ebb in volunteers and a program is becoming unsustainable. The Pastor shares with the congregation about the need and the possibility of having to shut down the program until volunteer numbers make it sustainable again. This warning is made for a few weeks, if possible. Sometimes additional volunteers are recruited, and sometimes a program does get shut down temporarily or permanently.

"How do you teach/encourage volunteers from the pulpit?"

- Preach that "childcare is ministry to the parents."

- "Make stewarding/equipping parents (not so much the kids) your emphasis. Kids can be wiggly and seem unappreciative. If a volunteer thinks only about the "satisfaction quotient" from serving in class on a particular day, it can be discouraging. But even when the kids seem unresponsive, volunteers can know they are helping the parents to be equipped nonetheless. And THAT will help the kids learn about God, too, as their parents have more to give their children and have been strengthened to keep on living for God, themselves."

- "Children are the church of tomorrow. Childhood is a rich time for conversion. There are more non-Christians in the kids' classes than anywhere else in a church usually. Children's ministry is a rich, gospel opportunity."

- "If you want to be a teacher/pastor/elder, start with the kids. If you can teach them well, you will be better able to teach adults well, too."

- "Among family-integrated church families, there can be a decided pushback against not only them serving and their children participating in children's ministry, but an attitude that is not charitable towards others who do volunteer/participate in children's ministry. Pastors said it was important to teach the difference between essentials and distinctives and showing charity to those who think differently from you. And, to emphasize that children's ministry does not have to a usurping of parenting authority but a very natural and even good way that the members of a local church to help equip each other as the Bible clearly tells us to do. The idea is to be a family EQUIPPING church. Not a family INTEGRATED church. Unless, of course, you are talking about the family of God, the Church."

- "Pastors can teach about children's ministry being a way to serve especially the mothers in the church. Singles, couples without children, and older members can serve the mothers (and fathers) who tirelessly serve little people all week to have a chance to learn and grow from God's Word. It is easy for those without children to take the opinion that "it's their kids, they should take care of them themselves" when it comes to children's ministry. Pastors can motivate these others to an act of service in keeping with the church covenant to help each other bring up in the nurture and admonition of the Lord those under their care. This is a vow to help each other... even with kids!"

Teacher Service Limits

"Do you limit the frequency that volunteers serve? Why?"

All of the pastors were concerned that member volunteers not miss too much of the worship gathering. They also wanted volunteers to serve regularly, but less frequently, so that they might have more volunteers with longevity of service.

Here are the common service terms in use:

"What are your typical Children's Ministry limits?"

Childcare (No Teaching)

- "Once a month." (most common answer)
- "Every six weeks ."
- "Every 4 weeks, would like it to be every other month."

Sunday School (teaching, but not missing the worship service

- "Every other week, because so few able to teach.
- "No more than once a month."
- "Teach the same Sunday each month."
- "Special teachers who just teach 5th Sunday."
- "8-12 weeks rotations of two teams AB AB."
- "Teach for two, non-consecutive months of the year, a month at a time."
- "Only women teach (Child protection policy). Once every 5 weeks."
- "2 weeks on, 1 month off—serve every 6 weeks."

TEACHER SERVICE LIMITS
Church Service Programs (miss all or part of worship service)

- "Decide by interview because still need so many volunteers, when reach critical mass, will establish. Influx and outflux of families in transient area make it hard to get there."

- "Every other week, because so few are able to teach."

- "No more than once a month."

- "Teach the same Sunday each month, special teachers who just teach 5th Sunday."

- "Teach for two or three, non-consecutive months of the year, a month at a time."

- "Serve a 8-12 week Sunday School term that lines up with an adult Sunday School course."

- "Once every six weeks/only women; all women; hard even those who don't feel qualified because the church is so small need them."

- "2 weeks, every three months on teams that wear t-shirts; add in a predictable schedule to help transitions between teams."

- "Use team captains to help teachers."

- "Teach 6 weeks straight, once a year. That's the lead teachers, plus they have various assistant volunteers who serve 1-2 times a month. This allows for training and observation."

"Customizing" Volunteering Frequency

- In one, small church: "The pastors/elders have an annual checkup with every member and see how they are doing. They might add or remove, increase or decrease from volunteer service, etc. based on spiritual needs."

- "We take into consideration many different aspects of each person's life: evangelism, family, devotion life, personal struggles, church life. Decide to change, add more, do less depending on how the individual is doing. Critical mass for a small church is 150. Under that amount, it is hard to cover all the "needs" of childcare."

- "This is a small church. CM needs as much help as it can get, but we still want to care well for everyone. That's why they decide case by case, how frequently its ok to serve."

Teacher Training

"How do you train teachers?"

The churches to whom I spoke, trained their teachers in some combination of these ways:

- **"We Mentor Teachers"** Pairing new teachers with more experienced teachers allows them to see a teaching model before they start teaching themselves. It allows them to try out teaching before committing to a class. As new teachers watch more experienced teachers, they can become familiarized with the curriculum and with effective teaching skills. This brings both greater continuity to the classroom and greater success among new teachers, which in turn helps the children learn.

- **"We Model Teach"** A seasoned teacher walks the teachers through lesson preparation before class, then has them watch him/her teach the lesson. Afterwards, they talk about what went well and what could have gone better. This give-and-take of loving criticism fosters an atmosphere of humility and teachability as well as helps everyone to become better teachers. As teachers (and perhaps even more importantly as fellow believers in community together), it is important to model soliciting, giving and receiving this kind of healthy criticism.

- **"We Observe and Encourage Teachers"** Watch and give helpful feedback that will make for better teaching and learning. Usually, this is something a CMA might offer a teacher who is feeling unsure of themselves or a situation with a child. It's not something forced on them, like the secret police and a surveillance camera.

- **"We Choose Teacher-friendly Curriculum and Give Classroom Behavior Tips"** One of the considerations in choosing curriculum that the pastors' mentioned was "how well does it fit our teachers and kids?" They might have loved a curriculum on paper, but it was not a good fit for whom they had. Others mentioned the importance of helping their teachers in managing a classroom. Even if the content is great, if the kids can't be controlled, the teacher will become frustrated.

- **"We Hold Annual Training Sessions"** Most churches hold an annual training session of some sort for their teachers. Some separated out training sessions for preschool teachers, from elementary school teachers, from middle school and high school, given the many developmental differences involved.

- **"We Use Over-sized Team Teaching"** This was already mentioned earlier. But to review, recruiting teams of teachers bigger than need to be on hand each Sunday allows you to pair more experienced with less experienced teachers. And, keep teachers fresh, since they know they don't have to teach every week.

- **"We Give Teachers an Assistant"** Some churches recruit teachers separate from assistants. A teacher might be asked to serve for a whole month, but have a different assistant helping him/her each week. This not only allowed for more people to volunteer with less frequency and spread the load, but also gives lots of prospective teachers to assist and get a feel for teaching. This can be a great way to make a good fit between teacher and class as assistants find where they most comfortably can serve.

- **"We Observe Another Church Using the Same Curriculum"** Many churches benefit from shadowing another church using the same curriculum as them. They can see it come to life and more easily see how they might want to adapt it for their use.

TEACHER TRAINING

- **"We Observe Another Church Like Us"** Some churches found another church of the same type as theirs and went to observe how they taught their children. This can be so useful for churches in unusual facilities, like schools, hotels, or homes that have to think creatively in terms of teaching space as well as CPP safety.

- **"We Go to a Conference"** Truth:78 holds a comprehensive conference each year that is a great help to many CMAs', deacons and teachers. Covers a wide variety of topics. Capitol Hill Baptist Church (Praise Factory) holds three workshops a year to talk about children's ministry issues and see the curriculum in practice.

"Any other teacher training tips?"

- "Don't just roll out a new curriculum and think that's going to fix all your problems. Every curriculum has to be fit to you. And will frequently require re-fitting as you change."

- "Pastors, speak with your teachers and check up on them. You are responsible for the teaching of God's Word. Touch base with your teachers to whom you are entrusting the children."

- "Pastors, visit or even teach in the classes once a year. The kids LOVE having the pastor spend that time with them. It also can be a great way to see what is going on in the classroom."

- "Don't underestimate the impact of the witness of a teacher's simple kindness and care upon children. It's easy to emphasize safety, then cross right over to the importance of teaching, completely bypassing the powerful witness of another adult Christian's love and attention in class can have upon the kids. And on the flip side, an attitude of "I don't really care" or "I'm just here because I have to serve" or unkindness can negatively impact children. Encourage teachers to simply love the kids."

Teaching Teachers about
the Gospel, Conversion, and Discipleship

"How needful has it been to teach your teachers about sharing the gospel, looking for true conversion and encouraging discipleship among children?"

In addition to wanting volunteers to be trained in the curriculum and safe childcare practices, the pastors I spoke with said how important it was to train the teachers about how to talk to children about the gospel, conversion, and discipleship. Here's their answers:

"What understanding of the gospel, conversion and discipleship, especially in terms of children, did you find at your church upon your arrival?"

- A number of those who came to a church re-vitalization situation mentioned how some teachers used a simple "pray a prayer" and pronounced a child saved approach.

- Some of these teachers even rewarded the child – in front of other children in class—a piece of candy or other reward.

- These were also the churches that had typically passed the children over to the pastor (and sometimes their fathers!) for baptism.

- Then, years later, all too frequently these kids either left the church or asked to be "re-baptized" as adults because they later realized that they weren't really converted at that earlier point."

"How did you teach your teachers the gospel to children?"

- "Providing a good, gospel resource for teachers and parents to hear and begin to own as they teach the children. Some pastors thought highly of "Who Will Be King" by Matthias Media, as well as "This Is the Gospel" put out by She Reads Truth."

- "Other great resources on sharing the gospel with children to give teachers and parents are: "Helping Children Understand the Gospel" by Sally Michaels; and "Your Child's Profession of Faith" by Gunderson."

- "Double check any curriculum used for how the gospel is presented. Teachers typically will assume that the gospel is presented well if it's in print. Sometimes this is not the case. If it turns out this is the case, and you decide to keep the curriculum, provide teachers with a better version of the gospel."

- "Make sure to help them understand the good news is for those who REPENT and believe."

- "Regularly sharing the gospel with the children---even every week."

- "Remember that most of the non-Christians in a church plant or overseas plant are the kids of the Christians present. Address them if they are in your service."

- "Train parents and teachers on the developmental differences of children which mean that it is prudent for a child to mature into their teenage years at least before making a public profession of faith, for the child's good and for the good of the church."

"Any wisdom on how to pray with children in response to the gospel?"

- "Make sure the gospel is presented clearly, but without forcing a prayer. Always encourage children to ask God to work in their hearts and help them repent of their sins and trust in Jesus!"

- "If you do pray with a child about conversion, do NOT make a PRONOUNCEMENT about their salvation. Instead, rejoice with them and POINT them to the next steps in the discipleship of continuing to seek God and ask Him for His help to live for Him each day."

- "Make sure to speak to parents about any prayer or conversation teachers have with the child regarding the gospel."

- "Encourage parents to speak to one of the pastors/elders about their child for wisdom about what to do."

"Any advice on how to avoid pressure conversions?"

- "Do not let any prizes be given out to children who pray to receive Christ."

- "Do not even hold up the child seeking to receive Christ as an example for the rest of the class, as an incentive to earn the praise of the teacher. You can ask the class to join you in praying for this child and for the rest of the children in the class, if this child expresses a desire to repent and believe in class. This is a good thing to do. It gives the praise to God while also holding out to all in the class that this is a free gift from God that He can give them, too."

- "Debunk the idea, so prevalent, that "If your child isn't saved by the age of eighteen, he/she is not going to be saved. This puts a lot of pressure to "force" a conversion. Teach on God's ability to convert adults! You will need to preach this over and over and over, especially if you are in the South."

"Any advice on keeping the gospel clear in the books you read?"

- "Check the curriculum for language that presumes that children have already heard and accepted the gospel. This is incredibly prevalent."

- "Also check any Bibles you use with the kids or recommend parents use with their kids. Most kids' study Bibles or devotional Bibles heavily presume conversion. Do not cloud the gospel with a false assumption."

- "Many Christian books, even by very reputable publishing houses, are written in such a way as to presume a child is a Christian already. Continue to use these good books, but with discernment. If it holds out promises that belong only to believers, then add the gospel so children can know how these promises can be true for them."

Baptism and Children

"What has been the hardest issue you have faced in Children's Ministry?"

- "Age of baptism, "proof of conversion," and readiness for membership."

- By far, this was where the pastors I spoke to had experienced the most difficulty within children's ministry, especially in church revitalization settings.

"What was the view and practice of baptism of children when you first came to your church?"

- "If the child is considered a Christian, his/her parents decide when appropriate to be baptized, but not considered members until 18."

- "Parents could allow their kids to take the Lord's Supper even if not baptized."

- "Some practiced an "open table", i.e., "If you love Jesus, then take Lord's Supper."

- "At another church, parents decided when kids would be baptized, not elders or church or kids. Kids were then baptized by their fathers!"

- "Kids, ages 10 and younger were regularly baptized."

- "Pressure from pastors on Children's Ministry leaders and teachers to fill a quota of baptisms for good statistics."

- "Youth being baptized at camps, then welcomed into membership with no further conversation."

"Is there a connection between baptism and membership, even with children?"

- "Matthew 28 is Jesus' command to the disciples to build His church. How? By making disciples, teaching them to obey, and baptizing them. The disciples did this and churches were the response. Believers who were baptized gathered and joined together as a local church, committed to submitting themselves to the authority and preaching of their pastors/elders and committed to taking care of each others' needs. These are actions of membership, not an intermediary step."

- "Don't baptize anyone who is not ready to be disciplined by the church, not just their parents. Make sure to speak to parents about this."

"What is the age recommendations of baptism at your church?"

- Only a few churches had a set, minimum age for baptism of 13. These tell parents to not even ask until the child reaches the age of 13-16. Everyone else, put a process in place that would certainly more suit the maturity of a teenager.

- Those who did not give an age cut-off said that usually teenagers 15 years or older would be most likely candidates to pursue baptism and membership.

- Usually, this was a long process. The long process helped to slow down and allow time for the child to mature. And, any child that continued to persevere was showing signs of true conversion by the very act of persevering.

- Pastors said they would be more likely to baptize a younger-aged child from a non-Christian/difficult life situation because they had already so clearly felt the tug and said no. But even in these cases, they would rather wait until youth because of the weight of responsibility of membership.

- Regardless of age, pastors did not want to baptize youth right before going to college. They called this "baptizing out of the church" instead of "baptizing into the church." This was frequently the desire of parents who almost out of sentimentality wanted their teens to be baptized before going to college. Pastors suggested these college students pursue being baptized and becoming a member at a church in their college town, instead.

"Who needs to be aware of the elders' position on baptism? When do you tell them?"

- "Everyone, but especially parents and teachers of children! Ahead of time!"

- "We give out our position on baptism as part of the membership process. We want parents to know ahead of time. Before we did this, there were a number of times when unhappy parents who disagreed with our position left the church. Better to tell them ahead of time and make the decision to go to another church."

- From the pulpit in the context of preaching on baptism in its biblical context, such as Matthew 28. The connection between conversion and membership is the big teaching point.

- In the process/after the church ratifies a constitution and a statement of faith that has clear membership guidelines.

"What is the process of a child being baptized and brought into membership?"

- "Not unusual for parents, with or without their child, seek the baptism of their child who have made a confession of faith."

- "Tell the parents (or the child, if with them) that they need to call to make an appointment to speak to the pastor, just like everyone else who wants to be baptized."

- "The child should come alone to this meeting. This is the first step in showing that they realize this is their own decision and this is a very sober and mature decision."

- "Have the child through a book on the gospel or discipleship (What is the Gospel? Greg Gilbert; The Walk by Stephen Smallman were books mentioned) with a non-family member. Again, the non-family member part is important because baptism ties a believer directly into the body of Christ and under the authority of the elders. Anyone being baptized needs to be known broadly among the other members as a Christian. They will be making covenant promises to love and care for one another."

- "Child attends membership classes on his/her own."

- "Membership interview would take place."

- "Pastor has important an conversation with the parents, making sure they understand that if their child is baptized and brought into membership then he/she comes primarily under the authority of the church and secondarily under their authority. If necessary, they will love their child through church discipline, if needed. If parents do not want this, then the child should wait until he/she is 18. If can't practice membership discipline, shouldn't baptize."

- "Child would stand up before the congregation and give testimony, just like any other prospective member to be baptized."

"Have there been any other baptism practices you have had to address that might be helpful for others to be aware of, going into a new setting?"

- A number of pastors stepping into a church needing re-vitalizing found the youth culture and youth pastors to have their own separate universe from the rest of the church. Not only did this show up in a separate church service just for youth, and sometimes led by youth (whether known as Christians or not), but also in matters of baptism. It was very popular for youth to be saved at camps or on retreats and youth pastors or camp staff to baptize the kids immediately. They return home from their experience, assuming that the church would also accept what happened at camp as a replacement for what would have taken place at church.

- I discussed this already on page --- but it's worth re-writing here how this issue was addressed by one pastor: "One pastor told me that he urged parents and camp staff not to do this, but if it were to be done, in order for it to "count" as part of the process towards membership, a video would need to be taken off the baptism, and the teenager would know that when he or she got back, he would need to go through membership classes, an interview with an elder, as well as give their testimony at church. He told me that these steps helped to limit these on-the-spot baptisms, and were a beginning down the road to them not happening at all. "

"What do you say to children who would like to be baptized, both those who are probably too young and those for whom it might be appropriate?"

- One pastor's words to his young son who wanted to be baptized, "Son, you are an American and I am an American. But if there's a war, I have to fight; you don't. Being baptized is similar to that. You may be a Christian every bit as much as I am, but you are not ready for the responsibilities that come with membership yet. When you are old enough, then you can pursue baptism and membership. Until then, I know it's hard, but keep growing in Jesus and He will be making you ready for that day."

- "The elders feel it is best for you to mature in the faith before you make this very adult decision. Once you are baptized and become a member, you will agree to submit yourself to the elders. Sometimes they will ask you to trust them with matters you don't completely understand. Being patient and waiting cheerfully to be baptized might be something you don't completely understand. This can be the first of many times when you trust your elders and obey. "

- "If they ask to be baptized, tell them to call the church office and make an appointment to speak to one of the pastors about church membership. Let them feel this weight."

- "Hold a special class for youth who are interested in baptism that helps them think through membership."

"What do you say to parents who would like their children to be baptized, both those who are probably too young and those for whom it might be appropriate?"

- "Waiting on baptism does not mean we do not think children in general, or your child in particular, can-not be saved."

- "Children go through developmental stages that allow their confession to ripen from heart, to mind, to will. When a child is a youth, he is in a better place to understand the commitment he is making, taking a stance against the world and for Christ. Waiting is for the good of the child, as well as the good of the church."

- "Baptism is not a matter of salvation. It is, however, the public sign of repentance and faith in Christ for life made as a person is publicly committing themselves to a local body of believers, as the apostles did. Baptism is tied to church membership."

- "Matthew 28 speaks of making disciples, which assumes it takes time, even for adults; especially for children."

- "Expressing the serious tone of membership when talking to parents helps them understand the soberness of baptism."

- "Sharing facts like these: 30% of adults baptized in a number of SBC churches polled over ten years had been baptized formerly as a child once. (i.e., they decided that baptism wasn't really baptism because they weren't really converted then.) And, 80% of kids baptized in those same SBC churches during that period walked away from the church as adults. Better to wait for the kids' sake and the church's sake."

- "If parents want their child baptized, one pastor would hold a special meeting on a Wednesday night once a year. He tells the parents to come and hear a talk first. He explains about the development stages of children, how kids can respond to please others, how baptism is tied to membership and children will come under the elders' authority, kids must attend membership classes and must read testimony etc. like every other prospective member. Most parents decide not to press their young child towards baptism and membership."

"In the setting of another culture, have there been other elements regarding baptism of children that you have had to think about?"

- Unreached people groups coming to faith: a number of pastors told me how important it is, in these cultures completely new to Christianity, to understand how authority structures impact pressures to be baptized. In cultures where whatever the father does, the children and wife must follow suit, it can be very difficult to immediately discern whether a child or wife is truly converted or whether they are saying they are, just because their father has become a Christian. In these cultures, it is more important than ever to teach fathers not to put pressure on their children and to wait for fruit before baptizing. This is just one example of how it helps to understand the culture in order to understand who should be baptized, when.

"What had been the congregation's response to the "watch and wait" view of baptism?"

- "Hardest for those who had been at the church before the pastor came. Some churches lost members over this matter."

- "Hardest for pastors who gradually brought consensus about the elders, then began to enforce it. The transition was not without bumps".

- "Very helpful when the position was explained in the membership classes."

- "Easier for the new members who joined after the policy was in place."

- "Better when pastors took time to speak to parents, sometimes multiple times on the reasoning behind their position and the good they desire for the child."

- "The passage of time helped as children who initially wanted to be baptized later lost interest in being a Christian; while others, continued to grow and show interest and were baptized as young adults. The congregation could begin to see the wisdom."

- "Better when pastors underscored that they are not saying the child is not a Christian, but is waiting for maturity to assume the responsibilities of membership that come with baptism."

- "At one church, a 17-year-old member was warned about his unrepentant sin repeatedly, then excommunicated. This is so difficult, but can be great at reminding other parents how seriously you view anyone's membership vows—youth or not."

"How have you treated children who have been baptized, either at your church before you arrived, or as part of new families joining your church?"

- "A common issue with military families who come and go to many churches and their children have been baptized at other churches."

- ""Hardest cases are those kids already baptized in another church. Should they continue to take Lord's Supper or not?"

- "Most pastors spoke to these families and explained the seriousness of membership and the tie of baptism to membership. Some families chose to not have their child to take the Lord's Supper and wait until they were older and were ready to pursue membership."

- "Some pastors, after speaking to the child and the parents, and seemed fairly convinced of the child's conversion, allowed them to continue to take the Lord's Supper until they were old enough to pursue membership, or until the age of 18, whichever came first. At that time, if the child (now adult) did not pursue membership, he should refrain from taking the Lord's Supper until a time when he could do so."

"How have you 'fenced the table' in regarding children inappropriately taking the Lord's Supper?"

- "Fence the table, but parents/families do what they are going to do. Some ignore your preaching and the position. Especially difficult in larger churches."

- "Some pastors and parents found it very difficult withholding the Lord's Supper from someone who may be a true believer."

- "Douglas Wilson" influenced homeschool families who see the father as the priest of the home have been found to be stubbornly "uncompliant" to the elders'/church's position. They think their view on what is timely for their children in terms of baptism, etc. trumps the elders' decision for the church. Pray for these families and for your elders to have wisdom in combatting the effect of this mindset within the church."

"What pressure have you or your kids felt regarding conversion and baptism? How have you dealt with this pressure?""

- "Pastors' kids! These kids (and their parents) can feel such a lot of pressure to be publicly recognized as Christians. It's almost as if some members think whatever soup the pastor is cooking up isn't working if his kids aren't Christians. A number of pastors, especially with churches in the South, received lots of comments... and so did their kids about when they would be getting baptized. Be kind and encouraging to these kids! Help shield them from these pressures and help them to come to a point of decision themselves. Receive the comments other members make with grace and use their words as an opportunity to teach them (again?) about conversion being a work of the Holy Spirit, even in pastors' kids!"

"Have members felt your view to 'watch and wait' on baptism means you don't care about the gospel and evangelism of children?"

- Families left the church because they said it wasn't committed to child evangelism because of delayed age of baptism."

- "Other families said that they thought this indicated that the elders'/church did not think children could be converted."

- "Avoid congregational strife by introducing the baptism position early on in the membership classes and teaching fully so they can (more likely) understand."

"Any advice on baby dedications?"

- "Some families still (perhaps unconsciously) view this action as having a special, significance in the future of their child becoming a Christian, more than other prayers for the child at other times. This can be heightened by extended family members from a paedo-baptistic (and especially Catholic) background. Help families see that any such dedication is more about parents and the congregation keeping their covenant vows to help each other raise their children in the nurture and admonition of the Lord. It has no special spiritual significance. Helps to move these out of the high-profile morning service and to a special evening service."

- The pastors I spoke to frequently encountered baby dedications upon arrival at their church, but gently and slowly down-played their significance and worked towards ending them.

"What Bible passages have been especially helpful to you in thinking about the baptism of children?"

- Matthew 28 speaks of making disciples, which assumes it takes time, even for adults; especially for children.

- Possibly Galatians 4:1-2. Analogous idea. As long as a child is an heir/slave he is under guardianship, but when is an adult, receives his inheritance. Both child and adult are heirs. Only the adult receives the inheritance.

- 1 Corinthians 14:20 Another illustration of a child's thinking not being mature.

- 1 Corinthians 11:27 "Do not eat or drink in an unworthy manner."

- John 9/Matthew 2

- 1 Peter 3:21

- Luke 14

"Are there any helpful resources on baptism of children you can suggest?"

- Understanding Baptism, Bobby Jamieson

- CHBC Elders' Baptism of Children Statement, Appendix A

- 3rd Avenue Baptist Church (Louisville, KY): Childhood Baptism and Membership

- Biblical Foundations for Baptist Churches: A Contemporary Ecclesiology, John Hammett

Parents Training Up Their Children

"Do your parents understand themselves to be primarily responsible for the spiritual training of their children?"

- Most pastors felt that their parents now know they are the primary disciplers of their children.

- Most of the revitalization church pastors felt that a lot of the parents, when they took the pulpit at their church, did not realize this. Many parents saw it as their role to be "good Christians" but the church's role to educate the kids. (Thank you, Sunday School movement! Not!)

- Parents with very young children in the congregation tended to feel a lot of insecurity about what/when/how they are to train their children and often unsure whom to ask.

- Parents who were new Christians particularly needed help in understanding this role and what they can do.

- Preaching from the pulpit was the main way these pastors began to educate parents in their role.

"Have you found any resources that help parents help their children in the worship service?"

- "Many parents make use of the worship bulletins the church prepared."

- "Some parents bring their own resources for their kids."

- "The resources used at church were more likely to be used at home for an over-lunch discussion."

- Some parents were helped by resources like "Parenting in the Pew" (Robbie Castleman) and "Children and the Worship Service" (Sally Michaels, Truth 78) Pastors read through resources like these and handed them out as free book give aways. They gleaned ideas themselves for how to help parents and children as they lead the service and preached.

- "Reading the sermon passage ahead of time (at home) helps kids to attend better during the service."

- "One father regularly reads the sermon passage to his kids and had them each choose three words they thought the

"How do your parents do with spiritually train their children at home?"

- "Most understand, about 50% do anything" and "Majority know; most feel pretty helpless" were the two most common answers pastors gave me concerning parents training their children at home."

- Many noted there was so much guilt and comparison, especially among mothers.

- "Mommy blogs put a lot of pressure on women to be super moms, but not necessarily super focused on regular devotions and family times in the midst of trying to achieve so much elsewhere (big birthday parties, every sport, music and dance activity, etc.)"

- "Need help with bite-size pieces of Bible truths and understanding what kids are like and how to do it."

"Do your parents use the resources you give them or their children at church to use at home in family devotions? Which ones?"

- "Reading through the sermon passage the week before the sermon and discussing it each night."

- "Using the worship bulletin and singing songs from it in the week after the service."

- "Reviewing the sermon or what was learned in Bible classes."

- "Use Praise Factory take-home sheets, stories and music available for free download off of the praisefactory.org website."

- "Praying through the prayer requests from Sunday."

- "Praying through the membership directory."

"What other resources do your families use at home in their family devotions?"

- "Reading through a book of the Bible, little section at a time, and having the kids (starting with the youngest) make some comment from the passage. Continue all the way through the kids by age, then to the parents and end with prayer."

- "Read the Proverbs or the Psalms, one chapter per day."

- "Have an inductive Bible study."

- "Use a family devotional book."

- "Read through a Bible storybook together."

"Do your families sing as part of their family worship?"

- "Sing, meditate, and discuss the words to a hymn and its application for our lives".
- "Listen to Christian music and sing along."
- "Sing before bedtime."
- "Take home the worship bulletins and sing the songs they sang on Sunday."
- "Our church puts audio to many of the worship songs online for us to learn and sing them at home."
- "Sing in the car."
- "Sing Bible verses, catechisms or catechism like songs." (Sovereign Grace Kids, the Ology, Fighter Verses, New City Catechism and Praise Factory for example mentioned.)

"Do your families memorize Scripture or Scriptural truths as part of their family worship? Any particular resources?"

- New City Catechism app
- Other catechisms.
- Bible verses. Praise Factory, Fighter Verses (Truth:78) can be especially good for this.
- Teach them the gospel.

"Do your families pray as part of their family worship? Any particular resources or ideas?"

- Read a Bible verse/passage and come up with an A,C,T,S (Adoration, Confession, Thanksgiving, Supplication) from it.
- Share about their day and pray for each other and others.

"What do your families listen to/discuss to disciple their children?"

- Read through Christian biography or fiction together and discuss it."

- "Watch a thought-provoking movie together and discuss it."

- "Talk about the news. Discuss and pray about it."

- "Talk about their day at school and their life. Everything is an opportunity."

"How do your parents help children who seem to truly be converted or desirous to be a follower of Christ?"

- "Help their children who profess Christ to begin to have their own devotions."

- "Speak to these children about how to respond to life with love and faith in God and love and kindness to others."

- "Don't whip them with Scripture. Realize that not only are they (possibly) young Christians, but they are young people. Think of how slowly you, even though an adult, grow as a Christian. Does it help you to simply have more Scripture quoted to you as you struggle and grow? Yes, make sure they know how God would have His people live; but, how much it is by prayer, patience and much grace that growth happens. And, realize that a desire to be a disciple or know God can sprout up before conversion has actually occurred. Keep pointing them to Jesus. Keep fanning that flame and use your life example and your encouragement. But keep waiting for fruit to bear out that conversion."

"How do your parents train their children as they go through life?"

- "Listen in the car to Christian music or a Christian book."

- "Acts of kindness and service to others in need."

- "Talk about what they see as they go places together. Pointing out God's beauty or discussing situations they see."

- "Share about their lives as they go places together."

"How do you use your life to train up or teach your children about God?"

- "Enjoy your children and love them.

- "Setting and keeping priorities and commitments you make to your kids and your wife."

- "Live out their lives before their children, seeking to love God and love others as He desires."

- "Provide a godly example of what it means to be a husband and father, wife and mother. Love your wife! Let the kids see you loving and caring for her."

- "Have godly friends into your home and life, letting the kids see others who also follow Christ."

- "Discipline their children with tenderness, wisdom, and consistency."

- "Respond to the world with a Christian worldview and discuss it with their children."

- "Helping their children to grow in character."

- "Helping their children to be thoughtful and servant-hearted towards others."

- "Educating their children and preparing them to be adults."

"How can you use your preaching to spiritually nurture children?"

- "Remember: the preaching of the Word is equipping parents as well as instructing children!"

- "I regularly address people in church by name, including families and kids. I have found that this helps kids and parents feel like he cares about them."

- "Include children and parents in your application points."

"Any tips for using books to help parents spiritually nurture their children?"

- "Pastor book give aways from the pulpit"

- "Church Library"

- "Church Bookstall"

- "Reviews of good books in the church newsletter"

- "Once a year bookfair of great Christian books"

- "Booklist of great books (put on church website)"

- "Harder to help parents if you are in a culture that doesn't like to read much. In these cases, it will be largely up to the pastor to verbally teach the parents and to "hand feed" them from the pulpit. Sometimes, however, you can help these parents along by reaching the kids with book giveaways. There are a number of great books on the market that explain big, Bible truths in colorful, simple ways. The kids will want their parents to read their books. The parents will learn from the simple text, too."

"Have you used membership meetings to help parents think about spiritually nurture their children? How?"

- "Discuss in members' meetings what parents can do at home or in the worship services with their children. Review a resource or a book for families/children each meeting. If desired, you can even have a copy on hand to give away or to have available in the church library or bookstall."

"Have you used membership classes to help parents think about spiritually nurturing their children? How?"

- "Since it is the part of most church covenants that parents are to bring up their children in the nurture and admonition of the Lord; and many also include that church members are to help each other in doing this, membership classes are a great time to address this."

- "Because you may have family-integrated families join your church, membership classes are also a great time to bring up the children's ministry philosophy and how we are to encourage one another. Make sure to underscore this includes not presenting your view of children's ministry (or of homeschooling, which also often is the case with these families) as the only way that Christians should raise their children. Better these potential members decide to go somewhere else before they join, if they cannot agree with this approach."

- "Membership classes are also where most pastors make sure to bring up the elders'/church's position on baptism of children for parents to understand and consent to."

"Do you offer any classes at church to help parents spiritually nurture their children?"

- "Offer a special class in Sunday School hour on family worship that lasts a couple of weeks."

- "Have a "parenting track" during Sunday School that lasts a quarter or a half year."

- "Hold special summer classes that reviewed parents' roles as discipler of their children and gave them ideas of things they could do with their children in the worship services, at home with their children, and other common parenting issues."

- "Kids are, of course, constantly growing up. Advice a parent needed with a toddler is very different from the advice they need with a middle schooler. These classes can be a great way of reminding parents of the basics, but also giving them new advice for each new phase their child is in."

- "Even a regular Sunday School class on any Biblical topic can help parents be better equipped to teach their children at home."

- "Workshops for parents; Dad's/Mom's breakfasts to encourage one another."

- "Don't forget the power of preaching to the congregation as a way to encourage one another in deliberate conversation and care for each other. This can be anything from a caring conversation to a full-blown discipling relationship. Members help each other so much just by building each other up. Encourage this as you preach, pastor!"

- "Try to have parents teach these classes who have not just "perfect" kids, but those who have been good stewards of "tricky" kids. Try to choose older parents, even empty-nesters. They can have a better perspective that comes with their maturity."

"Pastors in a missions setting: Have there been any special issues as new believer parents learn to raise their children biblically?"

- "First converts, rarely both husband and wife. It can be very tricky to disciple kids with just one spouse on board."

- "One pastor wrote a practical catechism for adults to use with questions and answers tailored to the culture and their needs. This worked to catechize adults and kids at the same time."

- "In countries with persecution, need to teach kids about persecution and what happens if parents are arrested. Prepare for the culture they will be in."

- "Parenting: gather all the believers in the city together to talk about this."

- "The older the kids/parents the more baggage there is to unpack. Easier with 2nd generation who are parenting from belief, instead of converted."

Coffee Shop Pep Talks

"If you could go back and have a coffee shop pep talk with yourself, right before you assumed your position as pastor, what would you tell yourself about Children's Ministry?"

"Provide leadership!"

- "Don't let children's ministry run as a separate entity. Keep it under the elders' teaching vision and care for whole congregation."

- "Own the importance of children's ministry."

- "Do not over delegate leadership just to do more. Do less and keep overseeing it. Grow more slowly."

- "Just do this" is not enough. Model and entrust is what we all must do."

- "Don't be so slow to see the need and importance of children's ministry."

- "Top-down approval of children's ministry decisions is not to be underestimated."

- "Know that children's ministry is one of the areas ripe for division. You might not feel like you want to spend much time on it, but need to for the sake for the whole ministry. Do it quickly!"

- "I knew children's ministry shouldn't be an afterthought, but not until I got started did I realize what a big deal it is. Plan ahead."

- "Keep to your goals (volunteer limits, view on baptisms, etc.) even with pressures coming in from other things or people. They need you to lead them."

"Building a healthy church makes a difference, even with Children's Ministry!"

- "Church planting not using a healthy church model is so hard. Don't do it!"

- "Having a shared vision of leadership/church among the elders makes such a difference. Especially watch out for the members attracted to the family-integrated approach. They think only they should disciple their children and can often be quick to tell others that's the only right way to raise kids It is a privilege to disciple other people's kids. It is a joint responsibility of our covenant."

- "Church covenant and membership and a plurality of elders make it easier to make leadership decisions for children's ministry and for the church."

- "When you bring on newer elders, see that they really understand what it means to hold to the teaching on baptism/conversion or whatever is new. They might not get it as much as you think, and under pressure, this creates bad conversations and disunity."

"Teach about Children's Ministry and parents' spiritual responsibilities to their children!"

- "Start teaching on deacons asap. Deacons will help keep your church from burning out. But make sure to have limits even on deacons serving so they are well-fed and have times to rest. Three-year terms are good."

- "Churches of mainly new Christians will especially need regular teaching that they are their children's primary spiritual caregivers, that it might not be easy, but don't give up."

- "Primacy of God's Word to help you stay the course."

- "Teach from the church covenant the mutual responsibility for the spiritual care of the kids."

- "Clearly, regularly teach that children's ministry serves the preaching of the Word; not replacing parents, but freeing them up to be equipped which grows their ability to teach their kids."

- "Encourage parents! Family is a huge part of the Christian life and how to train kids. Teach them how to evangelize, disciple, etc. their kids and how to help them do that."

"Lead the Children's Ministry leaders!"

- "Meet with Children's Ministry Administrator more frequently and try to train her more as well as press in on how tired she really is."

- "Wish had had given more direction earlier on to volunteers who wanted to know how to help."

- Church Plants: "Have people who know what to do and share the vision from the beginning. Even for the first Sunday."

- "Get the right children's ministry in team in place from before the beginning! Share the load; plan to replace and rotate leaders off so that they don't burn-out."

Spend time with parents and kids!"

- "Would have been more present with the kids and to encourage leaders."

- "Once a semester, have the pastor teach kids in Sunday School, himself, to connect with them; direct exposure to kids helps."

- "Would have been well-served to connect more with parents and the kids."

- "Wish I would have loved the kids more."

- "You get far more changed by getting parents on board than by starting with pushing through a new agenda. And, by better knowing whom you desire (by biblical theory) to serve, you will probably do a better job in actually helping those families understand and desire those biblical practices."

"Youth Ministry is extrememly important and can be extrememly difficult to navigate. Tread carefully; think strategically!"

- "Youth ministry is a very big deal. And changing the ideal away from entertainment excitement to the attractiveness of the gospel was unheard of. The old members had no category for a church this size without a youth pastor. They couldn't imagine. A specialty pastor is a must in their culture."

- "I would have come with more compassion for what it is like to be a parent of teenagers—so hard! Would have been much less judgmental for going to a different church because of a better youth group."

- "Ministry may come in unusual ways: youth ministry for teenage girls who join in the women's Bible study for all the women and learn and love it."

- "Youth group come when youth grow up in the church. It may take years before you have a youth group. But if families stay, it will eventually happen. Youth groups can be wonderful places for your teens to maybe find Christian friends, but more likely, have leaders who are godly men and women living out their lives and be available to get to know. These leaders can be instrumental in providing additional wisdom to what their parents give, and sometimes are more easily taken on board, simply because it wasn't the parents who said it."

"Cast a new vision for the church and for parents."

- "The old structures and vision needed to die, but it was so hard. Don't give in or give up. Just keep teaching and keep changing slowly but surely and gently."

- "I started out with affirmations and denials of what we believe: we are not going to do this or that. Would have been better to give them a positive vision."

- "Keep the worship gathering primary. Bring kids up in the gathering; train kids in children's ministry for the gathering. Help parents be equipped in the gathering; help parents be equipped to take the "gathering" home to be able to use what they've learned with their children."

- "Children's ministry should supplement not substitute for parents. Choose programs that support parents and children with classes that prepare for families to gather together at church and grow together at home. Try to enrich and enhance, not distract or detract from the gathering at church and the gathering at home."

"Create a new structure, but be patient. Teach before you change, if possible."

- "Strive to get ahead of the children's ministry curve. Plan ahead. Kids do nothing but grow up! Think about what they will need next. Look at any "clumps" of kids you have. Realize that this clump will shift upward each year. On top of that, you will very likely have growth from new families."

- "Create a simple but easily expandable model to be able to cater to visitors, since that's the bread and butter of a church plant."

- "Try to build a children's ministry program that is: Pleasant, predictable and a place to meet people. Do what you can to make serving in children's ministry a joy for your volunteers to serve: good curriculum, predictable, regular schedules, supplies in place, all help. Encourage volunteers about the opportunity to not just share the gospel with the children and support parents, but to get to better know each other by serving together."

- "Don't change too much until you have the right team to do it."

- "Beg, borrow, and steal ideas from others. There's a lot of good stuff you don't have to create yourself. Only need to shape."

- "Church Planters in Borrowed/Rented Facilities: Be prepared for how hard it is to have children's ministry without walls and without storage space. It feels very nomadic, and it takes a lot more work to set up. Getting volunteers who will help with set up and take down each week helps teachers a lot. Try to think as simply as possible."

"Get a Child Protection Policy in place and keep it up to date."

- "Don't do anything with kids if you do not have adequate safety measures in place for the children under your care. Church Planters: if you have time to only do one thing for children's ministry before you start, make sure that one thing is a CPP.:"

- "Changing to a CPP: tell them that it's good for visitors; make it a service-oriented thing, not a "we don't trust you anymore thing." It may seem awkward at first, but you will soon be grateful."

- "Adopt a CPP as soon as possible to lessen the amount of retro fitting of more rigorous policies on old members who may feel like the new changes are a personal affront."

"It is very important to spread a biblical vision for parenting and for Children's Ministry to other leaders and families in the church.

- "Send your leaders to conferences, such as Children Desiring God (Truth 78) or the CHBC Children's Ministry Workshop."

- "Be committed to teaching in right doctrine until the church wants to move. Bring the whole church along with you."

- "Senior pastors, when taking on new staff: train them carefully, especially in baptism position."

- "New elders: train them carefully and make sure they are in agreement on baptism position."

- Think discipleship: training parents and children, etc., not just structural change.

- "Spend time with parents."

- "Change can come more easily when membership, a church covenant, and constitution in place."

- "Preach on the church covenant to help show members how they can care for one another even raising kids. Use serving in children's ministry as well as deliberate encouragement of each other in conversation as helping fulfill the covenant."

- "Children's ministry usually is explosive because people care so much. Try to understand what they care about and preach/teach to that first."

- "There were so many battles at my church from the beginning. I wish I would have focused on training the leader of children's ministry and youth ministry and bringing them into the new vision."

"Set priorities for what you need to do first, since you probably won't be able to do everything you want to do immediately."

- "Ask yourself: "What is the goal? Who needs to be served?"

- "Look for safe first. Safe can't wait. "

- "As hard as it is, you have to have a children's ministry "thing" of some kind for families to come and stay. Try to make that thing fit what you have the best you can."

- "Look into the teaching: is it sound, heretical or moralistic? What is the approach to the gospel and conversion of children? What can you start to change through preaching? What absolutely needs to be changed now? What is the climate for change? If hostile, go more slowly and preach your changes first."

"Change teachers, curriculum, and structure slowly and gently."

- "Adding limits to volunteering helped a lot in removing teachers that needed changing, especially those who were territorial/would not attend service."

- "In re-vitalizing a church there are often sentimentality that needs to be gently dealt with, especially if doing away with old stuff or programs. Try to value these people and find ways forward for them to help. Help them catch the vision through prayer and through conversation, the greater helping the lesser not hurt so much."

- "Train more on the basics of how to teach kids."

- "Have lots of patience with those who don't get how to lead kids' ministry in a more biblical way. Patience, grace, gentle, God-like love for the people as you change."

- "If you have a transient congregation, you need to re-train every year."

- "You need to re-train as the culture, the parents, the church changes."

- "Children's Ministry Administrator: Find someone to do your job long before you plan to go and train them."

"Look for people like this to help you."

- "One overseas church plant: A volunteer coming from the States to take it on and strongly encouraging us elders to do something. She educated us and equipped us under our leadership."

- "Deacons/deaconesses are key to making children's ministry happen, especially with no one on staff."

- "A man wants to teach adults? Encourage him to start with teaching the kids. Great place for future pastors/elders to start. And these leaders can provide gifted teaching to the children. Win and win."

"Be winsome and wise with those who disagree with you about Children's Ministry issues."

- "Slow, sustainable change, within bandwidth of the church ability to change. Recognize that people who are upset by change are usually motivated by love."

- "Handle difficulties by talking to people before you teach publicly, bringing them along."

- "Impute good motives to those who are upset and act badly."

- "Preach the change and talk to people; assume good motives, even if bad decisions."

- "Older, long-term teachers are often the ones its harder to convince and change."

"Think about these things when choosing curriculum."

- "Don't just roll out a new curriculum and think that's going to fix all your problems. Every curriculum has to be fit to you. And will frequently require re-fitting as you change."

- "Incorporate catechism into the kids' program.

- "So much curriculum is screen-based and teachers don't really have to learn how to teach. Make the switch to actual teaching. It's so much better. It's a big switch, but a good one."

"Seek contentment with your limits."

- "God's Word does the work. You are dead. You are insufficient. Keep going. God's Word is enough."

- "Avoid the temptation of children's ministry envy. Look to your needs and your limits and be content."

- "Be ok with things not being all ok, just don't be not with them staying that way."

- "Make the most of what you have."

- "Do what you can. Expect God to be faithful.

"Choose a sustainable pace."

- "If you can't staff it, don't do it. And by staffing, I mean volunteers, not your actual church staff. I mean member volunteers."

- "Have healthy, sustainable limits on any service roles. This helps avoid burnout. And, you are tending the flock you have well."

- "Don't burnout your eager volunteers. Look for church to grow. Don't let it be through a children ministry philosophy of 'robust or bust.'"

- "Do what you can; don't do more."

- "A good structure of volunteer scheduling helps burnout; stick to your limits."

- "One of the best ways to get someone turned off by your new ideas is to burn them out trying to implement them."

- "Slow down, keep in control; do less."

- "Wait long and go slowly."

"Choose a strategic pace."

- "You might not be where you want to be, but do the best you can now. Add as you can, headed towards what you hope to have someday."

- "Think a few years down the road."

- "Be strategic. Don't build it just for "them" to come. and burnout for whom you have already."

- "Especially church plants need to build with flexibility since you never know who is going to come each week. Use curriculum that can expand to meet the new need in the moment, until you reach a new stable plateau and add a new class. This can help you keep the pace sustainable for whom you have volunteering, but also ready for the extra kids when they come."

"Choose a safe pace."

- "Don't feel like a failure if you can "only" provide safe childcare and no kids' classes. You are providing for the parents and that's a big deal. Don't burnout your workers."

- "Safe is a great goal. Don't look down on safe."

"Be careful with a change of pace."

- "Focus on accessibility of preaching the word to parents and add programs as you can."

- "Don't change too much until you have the right team to do it."

- "Have patience in looking for like-minded partners because if "I don't do it, it won't really get done" is no way to lead a children's ministry. The church must own it."

- "When you send out a church plant: It's always so hard to lose so many key volunteers when a church plant goes out. Always have to pull back and reassess. Offer less until more is sustainable. A regular pattern of ebb and flow. The cost of the gospel going out."

- "Shave off one year at a time when trying to add kids back into the worship gathering (that previously were in a segregated youth or children's church.)"

"Prepare families/children OUTSIDE the worship service to gather well INSIDE the worship service."

- "Teach songs in class that the children will be singing in the service."

- "Sunday is way better proactive. Help the kids prepare ahead of time by reading the sermon passage etc. during the week ahead."

- "Make sermon cards available so families can know what is coming and can prepare."

"Remember who your kids are, by nature. Help bring the aroma of the gospel to them."

- "Remember that your children apart from Christ are at enmity with God. Teach, pray, and be faithful, by God's grace."

- "Members can have a huge impact to the children in the church by their service."

- "Hard to be pastor's kids who are oldest and have no youth group etc. Find another church where they can take part. It's not a crime."

"Missions settings bring their own set of challenges."

- "Whatever your family does, disciple well, incorporate the regulative principle into your worship service; add applications for kids and make it simple enough that adults could take and teach their kids, too."

- "Teaching truths at kids' level to new believers/cultures is great for them and great for them teaching their kids."

- "Catechism is key, even if you are writing your own. Don't forget to add in practical applications of the gospel to your particular culture. Catechisms are in the public domain. Pirate, re-word, re-shape."

- "Go slow to go fast. Sometimes this means waiting to do a lot more with the 2nd generation Christians."

- "It's a long, long process to go from a new believer in these cultures to pastoring with all the elements, including the parenting involved to be qualified."

- "Help the missionary kids by sending over young adults who can show them the example of living as godly believers. Just the example alone is so helpful."

- "Missionary kids deal with so much transiency, sense of loss. Help them and help their parents know how to help them through these hardships."

Snap Your Fingers: Instant Changes Wished For

"If you could snap your fingers and change something instantly in Children's Ministry at your church, what would it be?"

Here comes the pastors' "grown-up Christmas list."

"More stuff."

- "A church building."

- "More space in the worship hall so all can gather. "

- "Africa: More contextual resources, such as songs."

- "Sweden, Russia, Turkey, Spain, Brazil, France: More curriculum in native language."

"Change in elders' mindset."

- "That the elders wouldn't think of children's ministry as women's stuff, but realize that it's their responsibility and opportunity to teach the gospel and make disciples to their church, entrusted to hands of often many others."

"Change in parents' mindset."

- "Parents would understand the importance of their children being a part of the worship gathering."

- "Parents would take seriously their job of discipling their children. They would see the church as an equipper and support, but not a replacement for their input in their children's life."

- "Cheerful trust on matters of baptism."

- "Deliberate conversations of encouragement and wisdom-seeking."

- "That I could have three hundred dads so in love with Jesus that they talk to their kids about Jesus."

- "More contentedness: Live within limits happily."

"Change in members' mindset."

- "That members would see that children's ministry IS ministry fertile ground. That it bears great fruit to support parents and leaves a legacy of good rich teaching from the beginning. It is an exciting opportunity for the gospel in our midst every week."

- "People who shared the idea that it's a privilege to disciple other people's kids."

- "Grace for different school styles."

- "Grace for different views on family worship and use of children's ministry programs or not."

- "Contagious excitement for the opportunities for the gospel that children's ministry is."

- "More passion: volunteers who own children's ministry and understand the huge importance and put energy into teaching well."

"Change in members' participation."

- "The members would see that they are partnering with families as part of the church covenant. Their responsibility and their privilege."

- "Create a culture that is more thoughtful towards how much moms need a break. That older mothers/people to give break to those younger moms, etc."

- "More singles serving the parents; not just the parents serving the parents."

- "More intergenerational responsibility for training up children and teaching parents and taking part in children's ministry."

- "More men to take initiative in children's ministry."

- "More volunteers to be immediately compliant with the child protection policy."

- "More mature Christians who could teach."

- "Never have any more shortages in member volunteer needs."

- "More deaconesses!"

- "Non-staff person to do schedules, etc so the staff doesn't have to."

- "More skilled volunteers/load bearers willing to help pioneer a new program and help train others in it."

Part III
Appendices

APPENDIX A

Elders' Position: The Baptism of Children at Capitol Hill Baptist Church

The Baptism of Children at CHBC
-- CHBC Elders, 2004

We, the elders of the Capitol Hill Baptist Church, after prayerful searching of the Scriptures and discussion conclude that, while Scripture is quite clear that believers only are to be baptized, the age at which a believer is to be baptized is not directly addressed in Scripture. We do not understand the simple imperative command to be baptized to settle the issue, nor do we understand the imperative to be baptized to forbid raising questions about the appropriateness of a baptismal candidate's maturity. We do understand that the consideration of an appropriate age for a believer to be baptized is a matter not of simple obedience on an issue clearly settled by Scripture, but rather is a matter of Christian wisdom and prudence on an issue not directly addressed by Scripture. Though the baptisms in the New Testament seem largely to have occurred soon after the initial conversion, all of the individuals we can read of are both adults and coming from a non-Christian context. Both of these factors would tend to lend credibility to a conversion. The credibility of the conversion is the prime consideration, with the effect upon the individual candidate and the church community being legitimate secondary concerns.

We believe that the normal age of baptism should be when the credibility of one's conversion becomes naturally evident to the church community. This would normally be when the child has matured, and is beginning to live more self-consciously as an individual, making their own choices, having left the God-given, intended child-like dependence on their parents for the God-given, intended mature wisdom which marks one who has felt the tug of the world, the flesh and the devil, but has decided, despite these allurements, to follow Christ. While it is difficult to set a certain number of years which are required for baptism, it is appropriate to consider the candidate's maturity. The kind of maturity that we feel it is wise to expect is the maturity which would allow that son or daughter to deal directly with the church as a whole, and not, fundamentally, to be under their parents' authority. As they assume adult responsibilities (sometime in late high school with driving, employment, non-Christian friends, voting, legality of marriage), then part of this, we would think, would be to declare publicly their allegiance to Christ by baptism.

With the consent and encouragement of Christian parents who are members, we will carefully consider requests for baptism before a child has left the home, but would urge the parents to caution at this point. Of course children can be converted. We pray that none of our children ever know any lengthy period of conscious rebellion against God. The question raised by baptism is the ability of others to be fairly confident of that conversion. The malleable nature of children (which changeableness God especially intends for the time when they are living as dependents in the home, being trained in all the basics of life and faith) is a gift from God and is to be used to bring them to maturity. It should also give us caution in assuming the permanence of desires, dreams, affections and decisions of children. Nevertheless, should the young person desire to pursue baptism and membership in the normal course set out by the church, we will examine them on a case-by-case basis, with the involvement of the parents.

In the event of young persons from non-Christian families coming to the church for an extended period of time, professing faith and giving evidence of the reality thereof, requests for baptism and membership would be considered without the involvement of the parents. While all the previous comments on the nature of immaturity still pertain, the fact that such a young person would be doing so despite indifference, or even opposition from their parents would or could be evidence for the reality of their conversion.

Nothing in this statement should be construed as casting doubt about the legitimacy of the baptism of any among us, regardless of how young they were when they were baptized. Because they have continued in the faith into their adult years we assume the legitimacy of their initial profession made at baptism. The question about how many people have been baptized at this church in the past as younger people and children who went on to give no evidence of ever having been savingly converted, and what damage was done to them, and to the witness of the gospel through the church's premature baptism of them. It is our judgment that while there is some danger of discouragement on the part of those children who do give some good evidence of being converted and yet are not baptized and welcomed into communicant membership in the church, through good teaching in the home, and through the loving inclusion of the families in the church as we currently do, that danger is small. There is, however, we believe, a greater danger of deception on the part of many who could be wrongly baptized at an age in which people are more liable to make decisions which are sincere, but ill-founded and too often short-lived.

Two other notes in conclusion. First, we realize that this issue is an issue of great emotion for some, and we in no way are trying to lead anyone to disobey their conscience on this matter; we simply are trying to inform and educate our consciences from the Scriptural necessity of a credible profession of faith for baptism. Second, while it is not generally known among American evangelicals today, the practice of baptizing pre-teenage children is of recent development (largely early 20th century) and of limited geography (largely limited to the United States, and places where American evangelicals have exercised great influence). Baptists in the past were known for waiting to baptize until the believers were adults. Baptistic Christians around the world are still much more cautious than modern American Christians, often waiting in Europe, Africa and Asia to baptize until children are grown and are in their twenties.

APPENDIX B

Children's Church and Family-Integrated Church Models

Are You an Advocate of Children's Church or the Family-Integrated Church Models of Worship?

We see parents as the primary spiritual caregivers of their children. They are the ones whom the Lord will judge for the spiritual nurture of their children. We see all of children's ministry as only a humble support to godly parents; and, that any way we can help prepare the children in our church to gather well with our local body of Christ as one of the most important ways we support our parents in this God-ordained task.

We are agreed on the goal of deliberate, parent-led spiritual nurturing, yet within our church, we have seen that the way parents choose to best fulfill this task varies from family to family and even from child to child. And, we have seen that this variance is a matter of godly discretion. In other words, we do not prescribe one particular method, when there seem to be a number of godly options that bear good fruit. So, we encourage parents to understand the great importance of spiritually nurturing their children, both at home and at church. We offer various kinds of support to parents. And, we help them consider what might be the best way to do this for their particular children/their particular family. So, as you can see, we agree upon the mandate, but will not divide over enforcing only one particular godly method.

No one can doubt that children have many cognitive and developmental differences from adults: the younger the children, the greater these differences. Nor can it be doubted that there is a wide variety of spiritual maturity among parents. While some parents may be mature saints, many are new converts. They are hungry to be fed and eagerly welcome help in teaching biblical truths to their children. Teachers of children with this kind of parent often help teach the parents how to better spiritually nurture their children as well as teach the children, themselves. There are yet other children coming to our church whose parents are not Christians and may not even attend church at all. The teachers of these children may provide some of the only spiritual feeding they receive.

For all of these reasons, many parents at our church feel that they are serving their children best by supplementing their own daily spiritual nurturing of their children with special Sunday classes that convey biblical truths on their own level. This is particularly true while the children are young and the cognitive and developmental gap between themselves and the adults is especially large. And of course, for the children of non-Christians, these classes—presented on their level-- may be the best opportunity they have to understand and remember the gospel and other biblical truths.

And so, we endeavor to encourage and support our parents in a number of different, appropriate ways, helping them to raise their children in the nurture and admonition of the Lord.

What exactly does this look like at our church? It takes on a few different forms. We have some parents who feel that it is best and even biblical for their children to be taught only by themselves. Their children do not attend Sunday School or Church hour programs offered at our church. They feel that regardless of age or ability to understand the sermon or other elements of the service, they are best fulfilling their God-given duties by raising their children this way. These parents choose to keep their children with them from birth on up. But even these parents are not partnering without us. The sermons and other teaching they hear informs their own hearts and minds and helps them to better train their own children.

We have another set of parents who choose to partner with other godly church members to teach their children biblical truths during the Sunday School hour, yet choose to keep their children with them during the entire church service. They often use Sunday lunchtime to review key points from the sermon and church service with their children.

And we have yet another set of parents who choose to partner with godly church members to teach their preschoolers and early elementary school children not just during Sunday School, but also during all/part of the church service, too. The K-4th graders of these parents are in the church service until the sermon time (we have hour-long sermons), when they leave to participate in The Praise Factory. Some parents of preschoolers follow this same model, while others choose to have their children participate in their own teaching time during the whole church service. These parents feel that the quality teaching offered at their child's developmental level in our church hour programs provides a helpful supplement to their own teaching of their children. They do not see the teachers as usurpers of their responsibilities, but partners who are helping to lay a theological foundation that will help their children understand and be better prepared to gather with the congregation. Teachers are careful to give feedback to the parents about any behavior issues or spiritual conversations that might be particularly helpful for the parents to know about. We also provide take-home sheets and other parents' resources so that parents know what their children were taught and can engage with them about these truths at home. Teachers and parents also watch for signs of readiness to join the service for the sermon portion, too. So, even though a child is age-eligible to be in a Church Hour program, sometimes we encourage the parents to go ahead and begin keeping their child in with them for the sermon and see if indeed they are ready. Gathering together is always our ultimate goal.

Because of this, we steer clear of calling any of the programs we offer a "Children's Church." They are really just children's classes that we hold during the Sunday morning service. We want to reserve the name "church" for the gathering of the congregation all together. It is this gathering we are preparing all the children to join for the full duration, as they are ready, and certainly by the time they start 5th grade.

So, you can see that we have a wide variety of parents, all taking seriously their responsibility to be the primary spiritual caretakers of their children, but doing it in a number of different ways. That while we offer programs during the church hour, we are not advocates of children's church. And, that while we are always trying to prepare children to gather with the congregation for the entire service, we provide quality, biblical teaching during all or the sermon portion of the service, for the children of parents who feel it is spiritually beneficial for them to have that, through 4th grade.

APPENDIX C

Children's Ministry Past and Present: Know Your Roots

Section 1: God's Children's Ministry

You may know my husband as a preacher or a writer or a speaker; but, let me tell you, deep, deep down, he is a historian! "Look back to gain perspective on where you are now and to avoid pitfalls of the past" is a summary of his motto. Take those novel Nine Marks he's always talking about! He'll be the first one to tell you to look back, even just as recently as the 19th century (let alone all the back to the Old and New Testament), and there they are, all in practice. Those of you who have read "Church Polity" will know that. (And for those of you who aren't familiar with that not-exactly New York Times bestseller, it's a compilation of accounts of church polity among 19th-century Baptists. It might feel like a nerdy yawn written especially for church history geeks, but very instructive, even regarding some elements of the church's/parents training of their children.)

So, what did my husband tell me to do at the very beginning of this book? "Write a chapter of the history of children's ministry." Inwardly I groaned; but let me tell you, it has blown my mind and expanded gloriously my vision of what God has been up to from the beginning. God is amazing... and my husband isn't too bad, either. (Thanks, Mark!)

Beginning with God

In going backward, I came to the beginnings of the modern "Sunday School Movement" in the 18th century when first Hannah Ball in the rural English town of High Wycombe, then Robert Raikes in the urban English city of Gloucester began inviting un-churched children to a special school on Sunday using education as a springboard for the gospel. And, while we will get to that particular, very special turn in the history of children's ministry in a bit, to start there would be to miss its beginnings by a country mile. Actually, a country eternity, for children's ministry has its root in God, Himself. He has been involved in children's ministry from before the beginning of time and planned it out to beyond the end of time. His goal: His glory and the enjoyment of that glory by His adopted children as they gather with Him.

Perfect Wonderfulness Shared
In eternity past, there was only God, the Father, Son, and Holy Spirit. Together they enjoyed delightful, complete fellowship. God did not need anything or anyone else. He was never bored or lonely. Life was perfect; or, as I say in the Praise Factory curriculum, it was "Perfect Wonderfulness."

Fast forward all the way to eternity future. Once more there is God, the Father, Son, and Holy Spirit, still enjoying perfect fellowship, but now with Him is who? Lots and lots of people!

Revelation 12:9-11 describes the scene:
"After this I looked, and behold, a great multitude that no one could number, from every nation, from all tribes and peoples and languages, standing before the throne and before the Lamb, clothed in white robes, with palm branches in their hands, and crying out with a loud voice, "Salvation belongs to our God who sits on the throne, and to the Lamb!" And all the angels were standing around the throne and around the elders and the four living creatures, and they fell on their faces before the throne and worshiped God, saying, "Amen! Blessing and glory and wisdom and thanksgiving and honor and power and might be to our God forever and ever! Amen."

Revelations 21:2 tells us who they are: "I saw the Holy City, the new Jerusalem, coming down out of heaven from God, prepared as a bride beautifully dressed for her husband."

This vast multitude is the Church, the great gathering of all of God's adopted children, transformed and glorified. She, His bride purchased by His own blood, to be joined with Him in the Father's house (John 14:2). And from before the beginning, it was the Church, these people, God chose to wrap into the enjoyment of His Own, Perfect Wonderfulness, that they might together know, worship and enjoy Him, and know and enjoy one another forever and ever.

How did all these people come to be His bride? Why do they get to live in His presence enjoying these eternal pleasures? The history that falls between eternity past and eternity future gives us those answers. It is the story of God raising up and preparing His people for that great Gathering Day, from their spiritual childhood to their maturity. The story of their creation, alienation, redemption, adoption, sanctification and ultimately glorification, that God, the first and best Parent, and the first and best Teacher, would bring about, Himself, in His children's ministry to gather His Church around His throne.

Scope and Sequence of God's Children's Ministry

The scope of God's plans would extend through all of history and beyond. The world would be His classroom made for them. History, His lesson plan. His Word, His curriculum. The Church, not only the children He would care for and teach, but also the visual aid of Himself displayed to each other, to all the watching earthly world, and even to those in the heavenly realms. Priests, prophets, kings, and judges, His chosen overseers/under-shepherd and teachers in the Old Testament. Pastors and elders, His chosen leaders in the New Testament. The Father, the Planner and Provider. The Son, the Redeemer and Head. His Spirit and His Word, the inward Tutors who equip and empower. And every earthly gathering Sunday of local churches, filled with His children, would be a dress rehearsal for the Great Gathering Day for all His children, the Church, His Bride, glorified and worshipping as one in His presence, in eternity to come.

Having described the scope of God's planned children's ministry to His people, let's take a closer look at the sequence.

Planned before the Beginning
From before the beginning, God planned and chose a people for Himself. He would be their heavenly Father. They would be His children. He would provide for their needs. He would teach them His ways. He would provide for them lavishly-- all they needed for each day; good works to fill their lives; his fellowship and the fellowship of others. They would know Him and reflect His glory. He planned to create them in His image. He would give them a living spirit so that they could know Him, love Him, and have fellowship with Him. He would reveal Himself to them through this special heart He was given each of them, through the rest of His creation they would see all around them and through His Word. He would give them good laws to live by-- to live together in fellowship and love of Him and each other. Life with their Heavenly Father and with each other would be complete bliss.

The Fall and God's Plans
But God knew this Perfect Wonderfulness humans could enjoy with Him would go no further than Adam and Eve, the very first people. They would quickly discard it for something with a much more bitter taste. The tempter would come, and our first parents would choose to turn away from God and His rule. They

would deserve His just and holy wrath. And with them, we would all fall. Humanity's relationship with God would be broken asunder, and the cost of the reparation placed infinitely high, beyond anyone's ability to pay.

The Mercy of God
Anyone, that is, except God, Himself. And so, as our loving kindness to our own, defiant, erring children echoes in the faintest of ways, God, the most merciful parent, planned history to be a glorious demonstration of the unsearchable depths of His love and grace to His defiant, erring children.

"As a father has compassion on his children, so the Lord has compassion on those who fear him."
--Psalm 103:13, NIV

"But God demonstrates his own love for us in this: While we were still sinners, Christ died for us."
--Romans 5:8

The Planned Savior through Abraham's Family
Though they would not deserve it, He would promise them a Savior. He would choose a family—Abraham and his seed. That family would grow into a chosen people, the nation of Israel. Through Moses, He would give them His Word, filled with His mighty works, His sure promises, and His good laws. It would tell them how to live as His people and how to stay in fellowship with Him. He would raise up judges, prophets, priests and Levites, scribes and even kings to be loving under-shepherds to lead them and teach them. Prophets and priests would gather the people together to worship Him and hear preaching from His Word, especially at the Temple. Kings in the capitol would lead them by godly rule and example. Levites and judges in their towns would lead them in their everyday life.

Visual Aids to Remember
And everywhere, every day, God would weave visual aids of Himself and His Word into their lives and in the land He gave them. From the Promised Land, itself, to the feasts that followed the cycle of the harvest year, reminding them He was the Creator and giver of all the blessings they enjoyed from it. The great stacks of stones around Israel He commanded them to erect near places where He acted mightily on their behalf.

From the tassels that were to sway on the edges of their garments:
"The Lord said to Moses, "Speak to the Israelites and say to them: 'Throughout the generations to come you are to make tassels on the corners of your garments, with a blue cord on each tassel. You will have these tassels to look at and so you will remember all the commands of the Lord, that you may obey them and not prostitute yourselves by chasing after the lusts of your own hearts and eyes. Then you will remember to obey all my commands and will be consecrated to your God. I am the Lord your God, who brought you out of Egypt to be your God. I am the Lord your God.'" --Numbers 15:38-41

To the mezuzahs on their doors or phylacteries on their arms or foreheads:
"Hear, O Israel: The Lord our God, the Lord is one. Love the Lord your God with all your heart and with all your soul and with all your strength. These commandments that I give you today are to be on your hearts. Impress them on your children. Talk about them when you sit at home and when you walk along the road, when you lie down and when you get up. Tie them as symbols on your hands and bind them on your foreheads. Write them on the doorframes of your houses and on your gates.
--Deuteronomy 6:9 4

"Remember! Remember!" said God's laws at every turn. The circumcision of boys at day eight, that would symbolize their part in the broader covenant family from birth that would, by God's grace, later reflect true membership in the covenant family as a circumcised heart of love for God. The just and merciful laws that would teach them not to show favoritism and to not forget the poor and weak as well as the "do not touch, do not eat, do not wear" laws of Leviticus that made them distinct from the nations around them. The weekly Sabbaths at home or the great gatherings of the nation around first the tabernacle, then the Temple to worship God, hear from His Word, and to renew their fellowship with Him through the sacrifices.

And oh, the sacrifices! All that blood, day after day! What a very visual reminder of their sin and their dependence upon Him, through His mediators, if they were to be His people. All were to help them to remember the holy God who had chosen them and His Word which was to be more important to them than the bread their bodies needed to stay alive. To love Him and live for Him. To love one another. All of these would be part of God's ministry to teach His children, while at the same time, to bring Him glory in the heavenly world above and in the watching world on earth. to remember would teach them how to live to love God and each other. Remember! Remember! Remember!

Loving Discipline for Forgetfulness
And when they did not remember or obey, the LORD would use these leaders and these laws to warn them of His coming discipline if they did not repent and turn back to Him and His good ways.

"Know then in your heart that as a man disciplines his son, so the Lord your God disciplines you."
-- Deuteronomy 8:5

Discipline, they would indeed face, because they would indeed choose to forget and disobey, as their first parents had done before them. But in His Fatherly goodness, He would discipline them to turn them back to Him.

The Rescuer at Last
And in His Fatherly, infinite loving-kindness, He would at last send Jesus, His One and only True Son to save them. He would live up to His name: "Yahweh Rescues." He would come as the good shepherd, the wisest teacher, the perfect law-keeper, the truest prophet, the worthy high priest, and the king of kings. He would live the life they should have lived, perfectly keeping and fulfilling God's laws. He would die the death they should have died, taking God's just punishment for their sins upon Himself as He chose to die for them on the cross. He would die that Good Friday and on the third day, Sunday, He would demonstrate to heaven and earth why we call that Friday good. His death purchased our life. He would provide the final sacrifice for sin. He would completely swallow up death for God's people-- all who would ever turn away from their sins and trust in Jesus as their Savior.

"This is how God showed his love among us: He sent his one and only Son into the world that we might live through him. This is love: not that we loved God, but that he loved us and sent his Son as an atoning sacrifice for our sins." --1 John 1:9-10

Help from Within to Do the Work throughout the World
Jesus would ascend to heaven, He would send the Holy Spirit to live inside of their hearts, the good work of spiritual circumcision. The clean heart He had promised to give His people from the time of the exile. He would help them love Him and each other. He would help them live for Him from the inside. Thus empowered, He would send them out with good news to build His Church, the outworking of the new covenant made in His blood.

"Then Jesus came to them and said, 'All authority in heaven and on earth has been given to me. Therefore go and make disciples of all nations, baptizing them in the name of the Father and of the Son and of the Holy Spirit, and teaching them to obey everything I have commanded you. And surely I am with you always, to the very end of the age.'" --Matthew 28:18-20

From Every Tribe and Nation
This would be a kingdom of God that would burst with people from every tribe and nation. Not an earthly kingdom, as He gave Israel, organized around the children of an earthly family, Abraham's physical seed, generation by generation, and allowing any who would come to live under the law, but never including many who were not of his descent. No, this would be a heavenly kingdom, organized around children "born from above," Abraham's spiritual seed, from every people in the earthly family, those receiving spiritual birth at the hands of God's Spirit, then baptism as the outward sign of that inward birth. The foretaste of this kingdom would reside in the hearts of those who by repentance and faith put their trust in Jesus, with the promise of the great feast of the Great Gathering to come in the new heaven and earth when Jesus would return.

"Yet to all who did receive him, to those who believed in his name, he gave the right to become children of God. But to all who did receive him, who believed in his name, he gave the right to become children of God, who were born, not of blood nor of the will of the flesh nor of the will of man, but of God." -- John 1:12

The gates of this kingdom would swing wide open to people from every tribe and nation. The days of "They may come" under the old covenant, would now be "Go and bring in." under the new. God would enable His people to "go out, multiply and fill" all of His physical earth with His gospel and by doing so, build His Church in the spiritual hearts of men.

"The gospel is bearing fruit and growing throughout the whole world—just as it has been doing among

The Church Is Built
God would raise up apostles, pastors, elders to lead and teach His children His Word and His ways. But not only would they be taught by these godly men, but they would all, themselves, be God's holy priesthood, encouraging one another and seeking to present everyone mature.

"As you come to him, the living Stone—rejected by humans but chosen by God and precious to him—you also, like living stones, are being built into a spiritual house to be a holy priesthood, offering spiritual sacrifices acceptable to God through Jesus Christ…But you are a chosen people, a royal priesthood, a holy nation, God's special possession, that you may declare the praises of him who called you out of darkness into his wonderful light. 10 Once you were not a people, but now you are the people of God; once you had not received mercy, but now you have received mercy." –1 Peter 2:4-5, 9-10

"He is the one we proclaim, admonishing and teaching everyone with all wisdom, so that we may present everyone fully mature in Christ. To this end I strenuously contend with all the energy Christ so powerfully works in me." --Colossians 1:28-29

And His Spirit would continue to work inside them, transforming them into the likeness of Christ.

"And we all, who with unveiled faces contemplate the Lord's glory, are being transformed into his image with ever-increasing glory, which comes from the Lord, who is the Spirit. --2 Corinthians 3:18, NIV

God's Plans Accomplished, God's People Gathered In
Like this, God planned to build His Church up into His Son, the Head, helping them live for Him until His plans would be all accomplished and His children all brought in. When Jesus will return to do away with sin and death and this old, broken world order to an end and bring home His children to live forever with Him and feast together on that Great Gathering Day where He and all of God's children, now His fully mature, perfectly radiant bride, would, at last, see Him in His glory and at last enjoy each other and glorify Him, forever in a perfect new heaven and earth of His making.

"Do not let your hearts be troubled. You believe in God; believe also in me. My Father's house has many rooms; if that were not so, would I have told you that I am going there to prepare a place for you? And if I go and prepare a place for you, I will come back and take you to be with me that you also may be where I am." --John 14:1-3

"Father, I want those you have given me to be with me where I am, and to see my glory, the glory you have given me because you loved me before the creation of the world. --John 17:24

Hallelujah, what a plan! Hallelujah, what a God! Hallelujah, what a Savior!

The Children's Ministry Plans that Always Succeed
These were the plans of God from before the beginning. And as Psalm 33:11 reminds us, the plans of the Lord stand firm forever, the purposes of his heart through all generations. As God planned, He has carried out, and is continuing to carry out even today. And so He will continue to carry out until every plan and purpose comes to completion.

Isn't it marvelous to see the children's ministry that God has planned as He would "raise up His children in the nurture and admonition of the Lord"? And isn't it even more amazing to consider the great Gathering Day that His children's ministry is preparing them for? All history, all eternity, echoes with the unfathomable love of God for His children! And eternity will not be too long to praise Him for what He planned and did in parenting us, His redeemed people, adopted children.

"See what great love the Father has lavished on us, that we should be called children of God! And that is what we are!" --1 John 3:1

Section 2:
Children's Ministry in the Bible

But God never does just one thing at a time. His plans have layers of riches to them. So, into this amazing children's ministry program, God planned for His people not to just be children and students, but parents and teachers, too.

Children Teaching Children
Now, perhaps God created the children of sea turtles to know how to crack out of their shells, dig their way out of their sand beds, waddle down to the sea and swim away without any parental aid, but not so did He create the children of men. They come out of the womb helpless and needy, physically, mentally and spiritually. They are made to be cared for and taught over long periods of time by their parents. As they grow, parents teach them what they need to know for both life and godliness until they reach maturity. Perhaps one of the reasons God chose for human babies to be so dependent for so long is to use the act of parenting to help the parents continue to remember, learn, and grow. It's no wonder that this God who loves for us to grow and change as we learn, wove His people into the very fiber of His children's ministry, generation by generation, for their good and His glory. Let's look at how God uses His children to teach their children about Him in both Old Testament and New Testament times.

Parents Are Primary: Grown Kids Teaching Their Own Kids
As early as the book of Genesis is the parents' responsibility to teach their children about God mentioned. "For I have chosen him, that he may command his children and his household after him to keep the way of the Lord by doing righteousness and justice, so that the Lord may bring to Abraham what he has promised him." –Genesis 18:18

While this passage directly deals with what the Lord was calling Abraham to do, similar commands are given to all of God's people over and over in Scripture: from Israel as Abraham's physical offspring in the Old Testament:

"He established a testimony in Jacob and appointed a law in Israel, which he commanded our fathers to teach to their children, that the next generation might know them, the children yet unborn, and arise and tell them to their children, so that they should set their hope in God and not forget the works of God, but keep his commandments; and that they should not be like their fathers, a stubborn and rebellious generation, a generation whose heart was not steadfast, whose spirit was not faithful to God." --Psalm 78:5-8

And to Abraham's spiritual offspring, the Church, in the New Testament:
"Children, obey your parents in the Lord, for this is right. "Honor your father and mother" (this is the first commandment with a promise), "that it may go well with you and that you may live long in the land." Fathers, do not provoke your children to anger, but bring them up in the discipline and instruction of the Lord." --Ephesians 6:1-4

These are just two of over thirty biblical references urging parents to teach the next generation about Him. It seems clear: the biblical instruction and nurture parents provide their children is the root of children's ministry. They are the God-ordained, primary spiritual caregivers--disciplers.

Parents: Primary But Not Alone

But that being said, nowhere in Scripture does it say that parents are called to do this alone. Far from it. If the teaching of godly parents is the root of children's ministry, the soil in which God has ordained for that root to receive the nutrients necessary to feed its little offshoots is God's people gathered to worship God,
to be equipped through the preaching of God's Word, and to build one another up through fellowship.

Deuteronomy 4:10 "The Lord said to me, "Gather the people to me, that I may let them hear my words, so that they may learn to fear me all the days that they live on the earth, and that they may teach their children so."

THIS DESCRIBES THE BASIC, BIBLICAL MODEL. Let's take a closer look at it now.

Children's Ministry in the Old Testament

God's People Gather to Be Equipped and Led by Godly Leaders

The Old Testament model most clearly appears with the giving of God's law to Moses. Through it, the LORD instituted regular times of worship, from the Sabbaths each week to the national festivals each year. He instructed them in making the tabernacle where they could gather together and worship Him. He raised up priests as well as prophets to speak His Word to them.

Remember: there was no easy access to God's Word. Even kings were instructed to write down their own copy. (Deuteronomy 17:18) Hearing God's Word read and explained by these leaders; remembering and meditating upon it, was how most of the people of Israel learned. The ear was pretty much the only gate to receive what they needed to live godly lives and to instruct their children in God's ways, too. They listened to learn what God is like and how He was to be worshipped. They memorized to hold onto His laws that were to cover every aspect of life. This was how they might love Him and love each other; and in doing so, reflect His character back to Him, to each other, and even to the watching world.

Children Welcome

Assemblies were not only for adults. Children would have been present as well, hearing the Law read and explained, watching, and taking part in the prayers and songs. Seeing the sacrifices offered for sin and in thanksgiving. Resting from work on the Sabbath. Actively participating in the annual festivals (Exodus 12:24-28). They saw God answer His people's prayers and act on their behalf in remarkable ways. Even the use of acrostic psalms like Psalm 34 (each verse begins a letter of the Hebrew alphabet sequentially) would have been easier for the children (as well as the adults) to remember. It even directly addresses children: "Come, my children, listen to me; I will teach you the fear of the LORD." (v.11)

Land and Law

Abraham's seed was a physical nation enjoying a physical land filled with physical blessings and physical protection from the LORD. His laws required many physical regulations for life. All of these were to point and reflect a spiritual reality of love for the LORD and love for neighbor unlike anything they would have seen from any of the surrounding nations. God's laws were exquisitely different from any other law code of its day. The unbiased justice for rich and poor alike, native-born and sojourner. The care for the weak and needy. Laws for a distinct way of life from birth to death, from food, hair and clothing, to health and sexuality, worship at home and as a community, work and rest… down to the animals. When God's people kept His laws, the clear community witness made all of life a time of teaching about God and His good ways. When God's people lived by His Book, they would be distinct from the world.

Holy and set apart to the glory of God, for the good of the community and even as a display to the world. God's laws filled God's community with practices and symbols begging for questions, even down to the tassels that hung from their clothing.

No wonder the LORD instructs the people of Israel through Moses to "impress [these commandments] on your children. Talk about them when you sit at home and when you walk along the road, when you lie down and when you get up." --Deuteronomy 6:7

When the community of Israel kept God's laws, it provided a rich, living, three-dimension set of talking points about the one, true God who loved them and made them His people. Here was the regulative principle "Preach the Bible, Read the Bible, Sing the Bible, Pray the Bible and See the Bible" expanded physically out to every area of life. There was much for a child of Israel to learn as he or she gathered alongside their parents with the assembled people of Israel or even lived among them in everyday life.

Home School Teachers?
It might be easy to imagine the typical family in ancient Israel looked the same as our small, nuclear family units today. However, that was not the case. Generations of families lived in compounds that expanded as children grew into adulthood and got married. Daughters would marry and go to join the compounds of their husband's family. Sons engaged to be married would build an addition on his family's compound as the new home for his bride. Grandparents, aunts and uncles, nieces and nephews, servants and sometimes even sojourners would live together and share the tasks of life on these compounds. This would even include the instruction of children.

And it's important to remember that passages like Deuteronomy 6:7 were spoken by Moses to the whole assembly of Israel gathered together. This is a manuscript of a parenting workshop for parents on raising their biological kids. It was a sermon to the whole community that told them repeatedly to be deliberate in instructing the next generation. So while "Mommy Aschah" and "Daddy Lemuel" most certainly should have been taking notes of Prophet Moses' sermon, "Uncle Zechariah" who lived on the family compound, and "Rachel" the elderly woman on the next compound over, or even "Zechariah" the God-fearing servant should very well have been thinking of how they could help teach the children in their midst, too. The high rates of mortality of men, women and children, made it even more important for everyone to consider it their responsibility to help bring up the next generation in the nurture and admonition of the Lord.

World of Witness
And if the whole community was gathering together to worship God and to encourage one another to remember and live out His good laws, what a beautiful picture of God and His goodness it created! What an amazing illustration to the children that the God of their fathers was indeed the one, true God, worthy of worship and the fount of every blessing!

The Model that Was Mostly Just a Model
But the times when this Old Testament, Mosaic-law-based model was a reality were all too few. The people did not stay true to their God or the covenant they made with Him. Numbers, Leviticus and Deuteronomy are filled with warnings against following the idols of the nations. Most every other book in the Old Testament references the people running after them. False prophets, unfaithful priests, idolatrous kings

led the people astray in worship and in life. Sometimes they did not just lead, but actually demanded the people abandon the LORD. The Temple was used to pay tribute to Asherah and Baal or abandoned for the altars to these gods in the high places. Precious children who were to be treasured and taught in the ways of the LORD were instead sacrificed by their parents in the fires to Molech. The biblical model lay largely forgotten and as covered in dust as the law of God which told of it. The fountain of the Word of Life was replaced with broken cisterns leaking false teaching, or dried cisterns offering no teaching at all.

Where did this leave parents who needed to hear God's Word to know how to worship and live for Him? What was there to pass on to the next generation but lies and idolatry? Very little. Only when the LORD disciplined His people; when prophets and scribes preached God's Word; when priests revived the Temple worship; or when a king read the Law and enforced it did glimmers of the beautiful community centered around the Law shine for both parents and children to see and learn.

"Again, the Israelites did evil in the eyes of the LORD. They served the Baals and the Ashtoreths, and the gods of Aram, the gods of Sidon, the gods of Moab, the gods of the Ammonites and the gods of the Philistines. And because the Israelites forsook the LORD and no longer served him." --Judges 10:6

The Exile
The demolition of the Temple and the deportment of the people of Judah to Babylon was in many ways a terrible time for the nation as an entity. But it was a good and measured discipline in the wise hands of their God. The LORD sent faithful prophets with the people into captivity to preach to them. Stripped of land, culture and possessions, hearts were softened and repentant.

Through the prophet Jeremiah, the LORD warned the people not to listen to the false prophets who promised a speedy return and quick fix to their problems. They would be in exile for seventy years before He brought them back home. They should settle down and have big families (Jeremiah 29:6). And while there was no Temple, the people could still gather together for worship and to hear God's Word from prophets like Ezekiel. This exile would last almost double the forty years of wanderings in the wilderness before the people were allowed to enter the Promised Land the first time. This would have been enough time for most of those who came to Babylon in the exile to die, and their children and children's children to be raised up in their place.

Settle Down and Seek Me
This is what the Lord says: "When seventy years are completed for Babylon, I will come to you and fulfill my good promise to bring you back to this place. For I know the plans I have for you," declares the Lord, "plans to prosper you and not to harm you, plans to give you hope and a future. Then you will call on me and come and pray to me, and I will listen to you. You will seek me and find me when you seek me with all your heart. I will be found by you," declares the Lord, "and will bring you back from captivity. I will gather you from all the nations and places where I have banished you," declares the Lord, "and will bring you back to the place from which I carried you into exile." – Jeremiah 29:10-14

The teaching of the prophets watered the hearts of this new generation preparing them to return and rebuild the Temple and re-establish the nation. God is sought and found by those who seek with all their hearts. The preaching of God's Word will always be God's chosen well-spring of instruction for life and godliness among His people.

Return from Exile
In 2 Samuel 7:23, David praised God for rescuing the people of Israel from their captivity in Egypt: "And who is like your people Israel—the one nation on earth that God went out to redeem as a people for

himself, and to make a name for himself, and to perform great and awesome wonders by driving out nations and their gods from before your people, whom you redeemed from Egypt?"

Ah, but how much greater it was for the LORD to choose to rescue His people from captivity in Babylon, having broken His covenant over and over again. How wonderful was His patient loving kindness to them! No wonder when the people assembled together in Jerusalem for the laying of the foundation of the new Temple there was both weeping for joy by the young and for sorrow by the old. The young rejoiced to see the happiness of fellowship with God according to the Law renewed. The old could only watch this less beautiful building be erected with the deep sting of sorrow over the sin that had caused its fall and the breach in fellowship in the first place. (Ezra 3:11-13)

Structured Schooling
Not only did this post-exilic period see an attempt at a return to life under the Mosaic law, but also the rise of the first, clear case for anything like "formal, church-provided, education" for both adults and children: the synagogue movement. Most scholars believe that the idea of synagogues sprang up during the Babylonian exile among the Diaspora Jews where they could continue to gather on Sabbaths for instruction and community. They were not to be a replacement for Temple worship, but local "instruction centers" for the Jews. This showed even in their basic structure: they were always built facing toward the Temple in Jerusalem. They were established in towns where there was a "minyan" of ten or more men. By Jesus' day it is estimated there were over 400 synagogues in Israel alone. Outside of Israel, many synagogues were formed as well—wherever clusters of Jews stayed in Diaspora instead of returning to native Israel.

Society Central
Synagogues were hubs of Jewish community. Some were very large and elaborate, even including kitchens and rooms for communal meals, meetings and even some living quarters. Many had charity collection boxes. Some had libraries and study rooms. Here, all the people could encourage one another in living as God's people.

God's People Gather for Preaching and Worship
But far more important to the gathering community than any of those buildings was the synagogue sanctuary. This was where instruction in God's Law took place. It was here where the scrolls of the Torah were carefully stored in a special cabinet. It was here on the Sabbath and worship days, that Jewish families and even god-fearing Gentiles, gathered to worship God, sing, pray, and hear a portion of God's law read and explained, usually by a rabbi.

There was no "pick your own passage" approach to these Sabbath readings. The Jewish leaders created a lectionary to be followed, Sabbath by Sabbath so that the whole Torah (as well as some of the books of the prophets) was expounded on in order with synagogues preaching from the same passage. What a far cry these days of copies of the Torah to be read and expounded in many towns throughout Israel and neighboring countries were from the days of Moses when even kings had to write their own copy and when the Temple copy was lost, God's Word vanished but for the word of the few faithful prophets.

Sabbath School Throughout the Week
But the Sabbath gatherings were just the tip of the iceberg of the instruction that went on in the synagogues. During the week, boys ages six and older went to the synagogue school to receive instruction in the Torah, as well as learn to read and write. Instruction centered on memorization, which was particularly important since very few families/no families would have even a portion of God's Word at home. But the higher a student progressed in the synagogue school, the further away from anything

that looked like pure Scripture memory he got.

Because of these synagogues, instruction in God's Word was more systematic and more readily available all across Israel. Actually, all across the Near Middle East--wherever the Jews stayed in Diaspora instead of returning to Israel. Jewish and God-fearing Greek families everywhere were being exposed to God's Word more readily and more regularly. And now, children from common families, not just those from rich, scholarly or priestly families, were being filled with a depth of biblical knowledge rarely known before.

Fathers still bore the responsibility of training their boys after the age of six, but these schools were a great support to their efforts. Girls would get the benefit of the Sabbath day teaching in the synagogue and any additional instruction parents (usually her mother) could give. This instruction certainly bore rich fruit in some. Just look at Mary's Magnificat, in Luke 1:46-55. It is full of the knowledge of Scripture.

The Hedge that Choked the Plants
But unfortunately, the green plants that sprung up through the synagogues became increasingly choked out by the extra-biblical, incessant rules of the Pharisees. This movement developed in the century or so before Jesus' birth. The Pharisees' teaching multiplied and took hold of many synagogues. The hedge of protection these serious teachers of the law hoped their rulings would bring to honor the LORD and His good laws, had the opposite effect. They muddied the truths of God's Word and stripped it of its meaning, as Jesus would soon prove repeatedly in His teaching. But even so, the rise of the synagogue set the stage for the true preaching of the Son of God and the spread of the Church throughout the world.

New Testament: Jesus and Children's Ministry

Jesus as a Student
Jesus would have received instruction in God's laws from Joseph, and even from Mary. He would have participated in worship assemblies at the Temple, and kept the Sabbath and the feasts. It is also very likely that Jesus went to his local synagogue on Sabbaths for worship and on weekdays for school, like many boys his age did. One hint of this is that Jesus is called "rabbi" (teacher) by His disciples, the crowds, and even the Pharisees and Sadducees. Usually, one received the title of rabbi only having been taught by a rabbi himself. Even the passage when Jesus, at age twelve, is conversing with the teachers of the law at the Temple, is an offshoot of this regular teaching interaction between teachers and older, brighter boys who were allowed to progress through to the more exclusive higher education offered only to bright boys showing promise as future rabbis.

Collaborative Community
This passage also hints at the naturalness of community in Jesus' life as a boy. When Mary and Joseph first couldn't find Jesus they assumed it was because He was somewhere in the large crowd from Nazareth who had all travelled together up the Feast in Jerusalem. If Jesus had been a boy who was expected be raised exclusively by his parents, He would have been kept at their side. And if He wasn't their first thought would not have been that he was simply somewhere in the crowd walking home to Galilee. Jesus was raised in a community. Apparently, a very large one.

General Opinion of Children in Jesus' Day
The Jews in Jesus' day considered children as a treasured gift from the LORD (Psalm 127:3). Outside the Jewish culture, children received every kind of treatment from tender love to abuse. Under Roman law, a father could even command his son be executed by simple command! In neither Jewish and non-Jewish

cultures were children treated with public importance, as we might today. A boy was considered a man at age thirteen but didn't enter the world of public respect until age thirty. For women, this respect remained rare indeed even after the age of thirty.

Jesus' Interactions with Children: Included and Cherished
But in many ways, Jesus acted in contrast to the culture around Him. He placed God's importance upon them, both in value themselves and as a teaching example to the adults around them. We know that He welcomed and blessed children. And when the disciples tried to put an end to this, Jesus gave them a stern rebuke. He pointed to the helpless neediness of children as being a necessary attitude we must have towards God if we are to be His people. (Mark 10:13; Luke 18:15; Matthew 18:3-4) We know that children were present when Jesus taught the crowds in the open air (John 6:9' Luke 9:37-48; Matthew 18:10) and received His healing (John 4:46-54).

Children Listening to Jesus' Teaching
Children would have been present with their parents in the synagogue services when Jesus preached. Outside of these synagogue services, children were also present when Jesus was teaching the Twelve as well as the large crowds that gathered. Jesus taught those who listened to not despise but to welcome children in His name. (Mark 9:36-37; Luke 9:37-48; Matthew 18:1-10) These were words of encouragement directed to the whole community, not just parents: children had valued and were worth their care and attention.

New Testament: Children's Ministry in the New Testament Church

In very noticeable ways, the Old Testament/synagogue pattern of God's people gathering together for worship and instruction, fellowship and encouragement that then flowed out into the individual households of believers continued in the early church. Matter of fact, many of the first believers would have still gone to synagogue on the Sabbath for instruction in God's Word (see Acts 9:1) , or to the Temple to pray (Acts 3:1; Acts 2:46).

Synagogues Had the Scriptures
Remember: the synagogues were the local guardians of the Torah. The believers would not have had the same access to the Scriptures, but by memory in these early days. Children who attended Sabbath services with their parents like these could still benefit from hearing God's laws read and preached. They could have learned from the prayers prayed and the psalms sung. Observed the Jews and God-fearing Gentiles seeking after the Lord. It also appears likely that boys from these newly believing families still would have gone to the synagogue schools during the week.

The New Wine and Wineskins
"They are filled with new wine." Mocked some of the onlookers when Jesus' 120 followers burst out into the streets of Jerusalem, proclaiming the good news of Jesus in unlearned, foreign tongues to the crowds who had come from other countries to celebrate the Pentecost, the giving of God's Law.(Acts 2:12-13) And while they were wrong to think these men were under the influence of alcohol, they were right to think what they saw had to do with new wine. Only this was new wine being poured into the new wineskins of the church, as Jesus foretold. (Matthew 9:16-17) The Law, celebrated on that day of Pentecost had been fulfilled by Christ. He had ascended into heaven and sent His Spirit, promised to transform the hearts of God's people from the inside and help them walk in obedience to that Law as they never had before.

"And I will give you a new heart, and a new spirit I will put within you. And I will remove the heart of stone from your flesh and give you a heart of flesh. And I will put my Spirit within you, and cause you to walk in my statutes and be careful to obey my rules." --Ezekiel 26:36-37

Peter preached to the gathered crowd, "Repent and be baptized every one of you in the name of Jesus Christ for the forgiveness of your sins, and you will receive the gift of the Holy Spirit. For the promise is for you and for your children and for all who are far off, everyone whom the Lord our God calls to himself." And with many other words he bore witness and continued to exhort them, saying, "Save yourselves from this crooked generation." So those who received his word were baptized, and there were added that day about three thousand souls." (Acts 2:38-41)

New Covenant Community
Radical changes were underway. On that Pentecost, the circumcision that welcomed by flesh into membership in old covenant community built upon observance of the Mosaic law, was set aside by baptism which welcomed by repentance and faith into membership into the new covenant community sealed in the blood of the Lamb.

"A new commandment I give to you, that you love one another: just as I have loved you, you also are to love one another. By this all people will know that you are my disciples, if you have love for one another." --John 13:34-35

So, the Holy Spirit worked His fruit in their hearts, and it poured out into their lives for all to see:
"And they devoted themselves to the apostles' teaching and the fellowship, to the breaking of bread and the prayers. And awe came upon every soul, and many wonders and signs were being done through the apostles. And all who believed were together and had all things in common. And they were selling their possessions and belongings and distributing the proceeds to all, as any had need. And day by day, attending the temple together and breaking bread in their homes, they received their food with glad and generous hearts, praising God and having favor with all the people. And the Lord added to their number day by day those who were being saved." –-Acts 2:42-47

From Sabbath to Sunday
Sunday, Jesus' resurrection day became the gathering day of the church, not in the synagogues, but in the homes of fellow believers. Gradually these services completely replaced gatherings at the Temple or at the synagogue, especially as the Jerusalem leaders began to threaten and persecute Jesus' followers. These Jewish Christians were losing their old identity, but this was to find a new one in Christ, their Head, and the Church, His body. And God used the growing persecution they faced to send them out from Jerusalem to be His witnesses in "all Judea and Samaria, and to the end of the earth." (Acts 1:8)

The Church Spreads
They preached God's Word everywhere they went: first in the synagogue assemblies, already rich with Bible knowledge and ripe for faith. But also in the marketplaces, along the roads, near the pagan temples and even in jail. In Judea, in Samaria, in Asia, in Europe, and beyond, the Holy Spirit worked in the hearts of both Jews and Gentiles to respond with repentance and faith. Churches sprang up. Believer baptism continued to replace circumcision as the outward sign of membership into the church; just as the Lord's Supper replaced the Passover as the outward sign of the Lord's great rescue of His people from sin and death. Elders were called to pastor and preach not only God's Laws but now the gospel accounts and letters from the apostles. Together, they were called The goal: to proclaim Christ, to warn and teach everyone with all wisdom, that "we may present everyone mature in Christ." (Colossians 1:27-28)

Children in the Church
What would it have been like to be a child growing up among believers in times like these? Those from Jewish backgrounds would have recognized the familiar pattern of reading and preaching the Bible, praying the Bible, and singing the Bible so like the synagogue assemblies. But how very different to see the baptism of believing adults, instead of the circumcision of children, and the observance of the Lord's Supper (perhaps weekly) instead of celebrating the Passover annually. Children would have directly participated in these old, outward feasts directly. They were included long before they understood them. But now, personal faith and believer baptism was necessary before they could do more than watch the church. Circumcision of the flesh had no place. Only the circumcision of a new heart, born of the Spirit.

Believer's Baptism
This was an important radical difference. Jesus charged His followers to "make disciples of all nations, baptizing them in the name of the Father and of the Son and of the Holy Spirit, teaching them to observe all that I have commanded you." (Matthew 28:18) Making a disciple, particularly of children, infamously known in Scripture to tend toward folly (Proverbs 22:15) would take time. Now, they would wait and observe the church in these observances until they had believing faith of their own and the elders deemed them ready for baptism and membership into the church, themselves.

Parents Still Primary
As for their instruction, we see Paul in places like Ephesians 6:1-4 still upholding the parents' duty to train up their children: "Fathers, do not provoke your children to anger, but bring them up in the discipline and instruction of the Lord."

Children Addressed in Church
But also, directly addressing the children who were present in the assembly, reminding them to: "Obey your parents in the Lord, for this is right. "Honor your father and mother" (this is the first commandment with a promise), "that it may go well with you and that you may live long in the land."

Community Still Supports
And in Titus 2: 3-5, Paul tells Pastor Titus to teach the older women to "teach what is good, and so train the young women to love their husbands and children, to be self-controlled, pure, working at home, kind, and submissive to their own husbands, that the word of God may not be reviled," which points to the community helping each other raise their children well. Parent, pastor, and members were involved in the raising of children.

The Beautiful Witness
But perhaps most deeply affecting upon the hearts of these children would have been seeing in action the remarkable love these believers had for their Savior and for each. To see your parents choosing steadfastness to Christ over avoiding suffering. To see them choose the needs of their fellow church members over their own possessions. To hear the prayers of the saints, full of the Holy Spirit, praising God despite terrible persecution; and to see God answer prayers prayed in dire circumstances in the most amazing ways. When the Body of Christ reflects her Head, the reflection is gloriously compelling.

Summary of the Biblical Model

The basic, biblical model in both Old Testament and New Testament of raising children in the nurture and admonition of the Lord starts with the Church gathered.

God gave priests and prophets (Old Testament) and pastors/elders (New Testament) the primary role of nurturing and training up His spiritual children in these gathered assemblies. (Leviticus 10:11; 1 Timothy 4:11-16) They would read and preach from God's Word. They would lead in worshipping God (Nehemiah 8:2,5- 6). They would encourage the people to spur one another on to love and good deeds (Hebrews 10:24-25). It was here that children watch and learn from God's Word and from God's people in worship. It was here that parents along with all of God's people, received the equipping they needed. It was here where children who received the gift of faith themselves, one day, would come to be baptized and be recognized as part of God's people, too.

CHILDREN'S MINISTRY IN THE BIBLE

God's Children's Ministry: A Beautiful Partnership Between Church and Home,

God's People Gathered at Church: The Soil for the Roots

LED: Gathers under the leadership of godly pastors, the church gathers to worship God and love one another.

FED: God's Word is central to their gatherings, whether they preach the Bible, read the Bible, sing the Bible, pray the Bible and see the Bible in the sacraments.

EMBED: God's Word is used by the Holy Spirit to equip God's people to live as God calls them to live. God's people support and build one another up for these callings through their mutual aid and encouragement.

SHED (Light): As they worship God and love each other, they reflect God's character and are a winsome testimony to the unconverted in their midst (including their own children) and in the watching world.

SPREAD: That these, too, might become God's adopted children, knowing, obeying, and enjoying Him now and forever.

From the nurture and admonition they receive at church,
God's people are equipped to extend this to their homes and to their children.

God's People at Home: The Nurtured Roots Send Out Shoots that Extend and Reflect

LEAD: Parents are called to raise their children in the nurture and admonition of the Lord. Some of this will be as they gather at church. Much of this will be as they live their daily lives at home.

PRECEDE: They do not do this alone. Their ability to teach their children flows out of what they receive from the body of Christ. They are first equipped to carry out this task through instruction in God's Word, the witness of gospel-transformed lives, and the encouragement of the church community, gathered together.

PROCEED: Thus equipped, they take these home and live these out, to please God, continue to grow themselves, to commend the gospel, and to train their children that they might be "wise for salvation through faith in Christ Jesus." (2 Timothy 3:15)

SEED: They know that this spiritual care of their children pleases God; and is often the seed that God uses to bring their children to repentance and faith in Christ.

SPEED: Conversion is the gift of God and a work of His Holy Spirit. They plant the seeds, but God must make them grow.

Section 3
Children's Ministry in Church History

How did the church live out the biblical models of children's ministry in the centuries that followed? Let's take a broad brush look through the ages up to our day.

The Radical Church (70-310 A.D.)

Faithful Model of Church
Christians continued the model of gathering at church to worship God and love one another. Godly pastors fed the congregation on God's Word and equipped them for their life tasks, including raising their children in the nurture and admonition of the Lord. Members continued to encourage and equip each other, too. Children themselves sat under the teaching of God's Word in the assemblies and saw the reflection of Christ in His body. Those who received Christ in repentance and faith would have been baptized and become members themselves when deemed appropriate by the pastors/elders. As time went on, there was usually a period of special training in the central doctrines of the Church and scripture for those wishing to be baptized and join the church. Hippolytus (150-225) mentions a three-year instruction period in God's Word. Baptism and church membership were not considered lightly. It was known to sometimes be even a three-year process.

Parents Teach with Increasing Help from Creeds
Most instruction continued at home by the parents. Wealthier families might have hired a tutor to help teach their children, particularly their boys. Summaries of key Christian beliefs, such as "The Rule of Faith" and "The Apostles' Creed" began to be used widely as the basis for instruction. These were sometimes called "baptismal creeds" because they contained the truths essential to understand and be believed in order to be baptized. Teaching on the Ten Commandments, the Lord's Prayer, baptism and the Lord's Supper were also taught. With copies of the Bible as well as the gospels and letters of the apostles unavailable to most, these summaries were of great help to parents. In a few major cities, especially Alexandria, Egypt, there were "catechetical" schools that taught adults and sometimes boys and even girls, key Christian beliefs necessary to baptism and church membership.

Orphans Included
Christians became renowned for rescuing and bringing up thousands of babies cast-off by Roman biological parents. Roman law gave husbands/fathers the right to kill their wives and their children. Christians found and adopted these infants and children, bringing them up in their homes and in their churches.

The Power of Persecution
Persecution of Christians ebbed and flowed in severity during this time, but on the whole, it made the decision to become a Christian a very serious, even life-threatening one. This most certainly helped in protecting the church from many false conversions. Children of believing parents would know on a firsthand basis what it meant to count the cost to follow Christ as well as the power of the Holy Spirit at work in the lives of those who did count that cost to help them endure to the very end.

The Received Church (October 29, 312-476 A.D.)

Constantine Outlaws Persecution
Constantine's enthusiasm, then conversion to Christianity led to churches enjoyed not just a calming of persecution but positive, State support. Church leaders were even given "tax breaks" to make their lives easier. As Christ's resurrection day, Sundays were made a weekly, public holiday. Production of copies of the Bibles and construction of church buildings were encouraged and financially supported by Constantine, himself. By 600, the New Testament had been translated into eight different languages.

Leaders with Lasting Effects
Some very influential church leaders arose during this time, men like Augustine, whose view of salvation the Reformation would continue to appreciate centuries later. This new, welcoming climate helped spread the gospel even if simply by making going to church and hearing God's Word more accessible to many. It also fueled major missionary thrusts further across the globe with the gospel.

Churches formed in southern Arabia, North Africa, and Ethiopia to the south, across Eastern Europe, Mesopotamia and Persia in the Near East, throughout Asia and even into China to the Far East, and all the way up to Ireland in the North. Constantine also encouraged unity in important matters of doctrine by hosting, almost overseeing, the Council of Nicaea—the first ecumenical council of church leaders from every country.

Easier Access
The benefits to instructing children in God's ways would echo the benefits to the church in general. Sundays were now days of rest, making church attendance easier. More copies of Bibles meant more who could read and hear God's Word. And, as the gospel went out to new lands, more parents and more children could hear and believe.

Power that Corrupts
But unfortunately, Roman patronage of the church also did much harm. The State was given say over church matters that should have been decided by church leaders only. The emperor's favor of Christianity made it the popular religion. Many who were not truly converted sought and received baptism and church membership. Others desired to be pastors just to enjoy the special tax status, without having faith, themselves. Even truly converted church leaders sorely tempted to make the biblical message more palatable to influential politicians. This gravely impacted the purity of the church's witness as well as the clarity of its message. And as time would soon tell, Constantine was just the beginning of the hand of the State reaching over to control the reins of the Church for their own political uses rather than the good of the gospel.

Discernment Needed
But with the State's new influence over the Church, there were more occasions when the biblical message was compromised, and the witness of the body of Christ obscured with unconverted members. It made what parents and children could learn at church, as well as take home for further training, less immediately helpful and sometimes downright heretical. Thoughtful parents would need to seek out the godlier leaders and rely more heavily upon any of their own, solid understanding of the Scriptures to discern how to teach their children in gospel truth. And, when faith becomes a matter of assent to doctrine rather than an act of repentance and faith, false assurance of salvation becomes prevalent.

The Romanized Church (476-1500 A.D.)

Biblical Truth Undermined by Traditions of Men
From the fall of Rome to the eve of the Reformation there was a gradual evolution of the power of the Roman bishop and the tradition and false doctrine that were to be so vehemently protested by reformers like Luther. Pastor replaced by priest and mediator, conferrer of forgiveness and grace; baptism to wash away sins; the Eucharist, the actual body and blood of Christ; the existence of purgatory; penance and indulgences instead of repentance; acceptance of the apocryphal books into the canon of Scripture; Mary venerated as Mother of God and mediatrix; the Roman bishop as Pope, Head of the Christian Church and infallible; Church tradition given the same weight as Scripture; faith a matter of assent to a set of beliefs, rather than a gift of God shown in repentance and personal trust in Christ. All of these sprung up increasingly during these years.

Heresy's Unhealthful Effects
Where do we begin to consider the impact these false doctrines had on the health of the church, at large, as well as parents and children in particular!? Practically every area of Biblical truth was clouded by heresy. As goes the knowledge of Scripture, so goes the health of the Church. There were many who had false assurance of faith through dependence on the Church traditions rather than on Christ for salvation. How could parents live out or teach to their children what they, themselves, did not know?

Opinions Welcome Until 1547
Fortunately, it would not be until the Council of Trent in 1547 that all of these false doctrines were taught and enforced in every church. Some priests, such as Wycliffe and others, disagreed. Really, until the Council of Trent in 1547, priests could hold and preach according to their conscience on these traditions without being removed from their church.

During this time there were yet other men, who called themselves the Free Church, who pulled out of the Catholic Church completely because of the rising pressure to uphold these unbiblical teachings. Families who sat under the preaching of these men would have had the benefit of sound teaching for themselves and to pass on to their children at home, as in fact, they did. Family worship including memorizing Bible verses was prevalent among these believers. And, in local churches like these, the gospel witness would have been much more clearly reflected in the congregation, teaching the children by example what it meant to be part of the body of Christ.

More Bibles in Hands
In the early Middle Ages, monasteries took on the task of hand-printing copies of the Bible. Later in this period, professional copyists situated in university towns began to do much of the copy work. They would even rent out manuscripts to students who wanted to create their own copy.

Then, in the 1380's John Wycliffe, a priest in England, bucked the Catholic establishment by translating the Bible into English and distributing them. He wanted the common English people to be able to read God's Word, themselves. Up to this point, most people relied on hearing and remembering God's Word in sermons or in memorized verses, and these in Latin, not their native language. "Every Christian ought to study this book because it is the whole truth!" Wycliffe declared. "It helpeth Christian men to study the Gospel in that tongue in which they know best Christ's sentence".

At the end of the Middle Ages in 1450, there was an explosion in Bible manufacturing with the introduction of the wonderful Guttenberg printing press. Bible prices began to drop to levels more people could afford. All of these Bibles were beautifully illustrated so that even the illiterate could learn.

Traditions Tested against Truth

"Faith comes from hearing, and hearing through the word of Christ." –Romans 10:17 With the influx of more Bibles, especially with the advent of the printing press, the opportunity for men to read, hear, repent and believe, even when sound preaching became more scarce. This was especially true for Bibles being printed in native languages, like Wycliffe's English Bible. Parents might not get anything that sounded like the "whole truth" at church; but those who could afford to buy a Bible of their own were beginning to be able to get it for themselves and for their children. With daughters of these wealthier families more frequently being educated as well as sons, the possible impact of the written text upon all children grew. The Catholic church was not pleased at all with this development. But it was just the first tremors that were about to shake the established church.

Schools on the Rise

During this time, there were also growing opportunities for Christian schooling for boy). Gerhard Groote, priest, preacher, and teacher, was especially of note. From mid-14th century to mid-16th century, he and his followers, called the Brethren of the Common Life, founded hundreds of quality elementary and secondary schools throughout Europe. Boys first copied the Latin Bible, then memorized Bible verses that were incorporated into the subjects they were learning. These schools became a model for the schools of Calvin and others in the 17th century in Europe and even among the Puritans in the American colonies after that.

While girls would still only receive their teaching at home, the growth in materials for use in schools meant that better materials would be available for parents or tutors to use with girls at home. At a time when the Bible was out of the hands of many commoners and rarely spoken of in the Catholic pulpits, these schools were keeping it alive in their students.

The Reclaimed Church (1500-1730 A.D.)

Mass Production Is Megaphone
The Reformation began with a solitary monk nailing a hand-written list of ninety-five thesis the door of Wittenberg Church. But it would be the mass production technology of the printing press that would turn Martin Luther's spark into a raging bonfire of contention among Christians in Europe and would affect change across the world. The Free Church denominations spread and grew, but not without persecution. This was especially true of the Puritans and the Anabaptists in the 1600s. The many members of the persecuted Free Church denominations sailed to America where there was the promise of religious freedom, ushering in a vibrant period of Puritan churches and writings.

Free Churches: Back to Healthy, Biblical Basics
The resulting new Presbyterian, Lutheran, and Anabaptists "Free Church" denominations were a major turn back to the primacy of Scripture for life and godliness among believers. And, as the blueprint for church structure, church leaders and church life. And these changes were great for the health of the church in general, and as I would like to highlight, communicating the gospel to children, in particular.

Well-Fed Congregations: Preaching and Worship
The expositional preaching nourished congregations with God's Word. Membership based on repentance and faith clarified the gospel and strengthened the witness of the church and its ability to spiritually encourage one another. Congregational hymns were being written and sung as a regular part of services, not only in Latin but in native languages, too. Martin Luther translated the Bible into German.

Catechism Explosion
Luther, Calvin, the Westminster Divines, Isaac Watts, and others wrote catechisms for adults and for children. Isaac Watts even set some of his truths to music. These were distributed widely through the printing press. This made it much easier for parents to learn and teach Bible truths to their children at home. This was especially important since they were correcting the commonly held heretical views of the Catholic Church.

The First Sunday Schools
Sunday afternoons became time for Catechism School for adults seeking membership as well as the children of current children's members. These would frequently be led by the pastor. These classes supported the parents' instruction of their children and gave the pastors an opportunity to observe firsthand a child's maturing understanding of truth and readiness for baptism and membership-- something that did not occur until the teen years at the youngest. There was great care taken in not baptizing anyone until they were clearly converted.

The Empire Strikes Back... With Impact Even Today
Unfortunately, the Catholic Church fought back by creating its own catechism around 1555 as part of its written response to the Reformers (the Council of Trent/Counter-Reformation). This catechism set in stone the heretical doctrines that had been left up for debate until the Reformation. On top of this, priests were discouraged from teaching from the Bible. Bishop Hooper of Gloucester polled 311 priests during this time and found 168 "were unable to repeat the Ten Commandments. Thirty-one did not know where to find them. Forty could not tell where the Lord's Prayer is to be found and thirty-one did not know the Author." This was a terrible turn, for the Catholic church. Now every child and every adult in the Catholic Church would be receiving the full dose of these false teachings, yet very little teaching in the Bible. We see the impact of these around us even today.

The Revived Church (1730-1920 A.D.)

Revive Us Again
Life in a fallen world full of fallen people means the gospel must continually be contended for. (Jude 1:3-4) So, the great highs of the Reformation were followed not by simply a plateau, but deep dips into valleys even as soon as the mid 1730s. And into these lows comes a wave of revivals that would send shockwaves to the ends of the earth in breadth and even into the mid-20th century in length with the First, Second, and Third Great Awakenings, and in some ways, all the way up to today.

While men like Griffith Jones were forerunners of this movement, it was primarily the preaching of John Wesley and George Whitefield that stoked the revival fires in the First Great Awakening. Their preaching from Church of England pulpits emphasized true conversion and holiness and revitalized many already in the pews. Their open-air preaching to thousands upon thousands of unchurched people brought many to repentance and faith as well. Converts were urged to join a local church as well as attend the local "Holy Club." While this may have been the pattern at first, it would gradually lead to the formation of the Methodist Church as its own, separate denomination.

Holiness Helps
For the truly converted who followed through by going to church, the outcome was encouraging. Change of heart equipped by regular biblical preaching from the pulpit, and fellow members to live a life of godliness would in turn help create a change in the home, too. Bringing their children to the regular children's catechism time on Sunday afternoons with pastors helped these new Christian parents teach their children what they were only learning themselves. Family worship times were encouraged and included bible reading, hymn singing and heart-felt, extemporaneous prayers. The testimony of parents seeking to live their lives in holiness did not go unnoticed by their children.

Holiness Holes
But there were problems with conversions from these open-air gatherings, too. There was no congregation surrounding these new converts to wrap them into church life or make sure they truly understood the gospel. Conversion could be seen as something separate from discipleship and church membership. It would be easy to simply live a "personal faith" and not go to church. We still see the sad effects of this even today.

Three Waves
The Methodists dominated Revivalism in the First Great Awakening, but especially in the Second and Third Great Awakenings, were not alone. Lyman Beecher (Presbyterian) and Asahel Nettleton (Congregationalist) as well as staunch Arminian-Presbyterian-gone-astray Charles Finney would be important names in the Second Great Awakening. Holiness preacher D.L Moody to Salvation Army William Booth (and in some ways, even up Baptist Billy Graham), in the Third.

Modern Machines Multiply the Good and the Bad
20th-century leaps in transportation (trains, planes, and automobiles) and in communication (radio, television, and the internet) significantly increased the impact of these men's ministry. The gospel message could reach millions at a time. But because of the "down-grade" of the gospel shared, which significantly lessened the tie of conversion to discipleship and discipleship to membership at the local church. Many people could say they "prayed a prayer" and receive assurance of faith that was not theirs to have. The consistent, solid teaching and body life so important to both recognize true conversion and to persevere in discipleship was increasingly missing. The attention to the theology and church history which had reformed the church was increasingly replaced with emphasis on experience as well

as Arminianism and Dispensationalism. The process of church membership by careful examination of each believers would be something only a minority of churches would retain. This was not only terrible for the individuals involved, but also for their ability to know, teach and raise up children in true Christian instruction. It was terrible for the pure witness of the church.

Gospel Gimmicks
Men like D.L. Moody offered children candy and pony rides as an opportunity to tell them the gospel. Moody would add pragmatism to revivalism, the ends justifying the means. "Practical solutions to spiritual problems." And, "If you can make a man believe you truly love him, you have won him," he was known to say. But were the responses to his message for love of God and hatred of sin or love of fun and hatred of boredom?

Keep It Simple, Keep It Easy
Belief, without the mention of repentance or waiting for the fruit of repentance, became increasingly the gospel going around, thanks in part to revivalism. Both conversion and church membership in some churches would slide from careful catechism and membership classes of the Reformation and Puritan eras to just a walk down the aisle and a handshake which is not infrequently the case even today. This was enough for the revivalists. Why should churches make it any "harder"?

This "easy believe-ism" has it's been called was an especially bad idea with children. Many children sincerely are converted at a young age, but many may be persuaded to pray a prayer out of love of parent or teacher or pressure from peers. All children are best served by adults taking seriously their seeking God, but wait for maturity in thought, consistency in discipleship, perseverance in trial and readiness for the duties of membership before baptizing. The storms of young adulthood often are enough to clarify true conversion from false conversion.. This was the rule of thumb in baptistic churches for centuries but was increasingly discarded during this period, as it is largely forgotten, even today. Baptism numbers soared as baptismal ages dropped as a result. Sadly, many of these children would go on to abandon their childhood faith as they grew up or ask to be "re-baptized" as an adult when they were of the age to truly feel the tug of the world, turn away to put their faith in Christ authentically. This is one wave of revivalism that still is lapping the shores of many baptistic churches even today.

Reaching the Unreached
This newfound fervor fueled many new outreaches to the unreached. The neglected and over-worked in cities; the American pioneers pushing their way to the West; the African slaves; and peoples in faraway lands where the gospel had never gone were all of particular concern. Each of these groups included children and often received special attention.

Unreached around the World
Missionary societies sprung up and trained many to take the gospel to foreign lands. How and who trained them made a huge difference in how churches were established in these new places. Men like John Paton did this well. "Take the gospel; write down the Bible; teach the people; establish churches" was the model he used, reflecting the Matthew 28 mandate to make disciples and baptize them, teaching them to obey. The lives of adults and children in new parts of the world were being transformed by the preaching of the gospel. Learning to read the Bible in their own language gave these new churches the tools they needed to equip parents and children for worship in church as well as life at home.

Unreached Streets
Care for orphans had long been a hallmark of the Christian church, but during this era, there were a number of men throughout Europe who impacted thousands of orphans. George Muller of Bristol,

England is especially of note. These men tended to the physical needs of the children and educated them with an eye for the gospel and the good of society. Not only were they taught the Bible in class, but they witnessed the living God whose Word it was in the lives of fervent prayer and joyful dependence upon an amazing, prayer-answering God every day. When a child was old enough to leave the orphanage, Muller placed a Bible in his right hand and a coin in his left hand. Telling them to "hold on to the teaching in that book and you will always have something for your left hand to hold." 10,000+ children came and left through the doors of Mueller's orphanage. All were heard the gospel and learned the Bible. Many were converted and became church members. Some pastors and missionaries.

Sunday Schools: Unreached Unchurched

The Sunday School Movement was a product of these times, too. While there were others before him, Robert Raikes' outreach to non-Christian children in the slums of Gloucester, England in 1757 was one of the most important catalysts. These first "Sunday School" classes were held on Sunday because this was the only day off for these children who worked in factories the other six days of the week.

At Raikes' Sunday School, boys and girls were not only taught a catechism of Bible truth and taken to church but were also taught how to read (and write). This would be the only formal instruction many of these children would ever receive. Raikes' goals were moral and spiritual in nature. He hoped that these classes would not only bring the gospel to these children, but in doing so, might also stem the staggering rise in crime and immorality in his city that was tied to these unchurched, unschooled children when they grew up.

Surprising Results

Though controversial among Sabbatarians who saw these schools as work, rather than an act of mercy and an aid to worship, the classes were nonetheless hugely successful and spread throughout the rest of Great Britain. By 1831 it is estimated that over a million children attended Sunday School weekly in England—a staggering 25% of the population. Sunday Schools were frequently held in homes and were often taught by women. Some of these women were volunteers, some were paid. This appears to be the first time that women played a regular, major teaching role in children's Christian education outside of the home or the convent. Women, even today, are still often the ones providing this role in children's Sunday School classes in churches.

Public Education Brings Changes to Sunday School

In 1870, public education for all children was legislated in Great Britain. From this time, Sunday Schools gradually came to focus only on Bible teaching, as well as increasingly included the children from church member families, more like what we find in churches today.

The goals were to:
- to share the gospel that the lost might be saved
- to make disciples of all who trust in Christ
- to supplement any Bible teaching parents provided at home and to provide such teaching for children without Christian parents at home
- to provide children with a testimony of life with God in the lives of their teachers
- to leave a legacy of Bible truths and knowledge of Scripture in the minds
- to prepare them to gather together in worship with the members of a local church.

Sunday School Shift

By the 1900s, Sunday School hour was changing, too. Now they were for not only the unchurched children but for the children of church members, too. They became dual purpose: bringing gospel truths to those who would never hear them at home and reinforcing gospel truths to those whose parents did.

Sunday School continued to be held before the church worship service during this time. This not only created an opportunity for there to be classes for adults to be going on at the same time as the children's classes, but it held onto the idea that the worship service was the main point of the Sunday gathering.

Sunday School Spread and Systematized

Sunday Schools began in England, but their popularity and influence quickly spread, especially to America. And by going to America, it would be institutionalized by the "Sunday School Boards" of many denominations in the late 1800s that would each be churning out the first special, graded curriculum for children in their churches in Sunday Schools, followed by special occasion curriculum, such as Vacation Bible Schools, by the end of the 19th-century. These establishments would be writing the Bible teaching script for teachers of millions of children in each denomination. The majority of churches in the United States still rely heavily on them.

Child-centered Teaching Influences Curriculum Dramatically

The early days of catechism-based Sunday School was changing during this time, too. Influencing this trend was the rising popularity of "child-centered" teaching. While John Comenius (1592-1670) ushered in the modern era of developmentally friendly, "child-centered" teaching years earlier, it was in the early 20th-century that this philosophy of education was very much coming of age. These included ideas like: "Children are children. They aren't little adults. They need teaching that is appropriate for them. Education must be pleasant to be effective. Children of similar ages should be grouped together so they can best understand what is being taught. Multi-sensory activities are the most beneficial means of teaching. Even play is educational."

All of these teaching concepts, which seem so very modern to us, actually have their roots centuries ago in this man. John Dewey's writings at the turn of the 20th-century catapulted Comenius' thought to the forefront of the public education front where it has held a leading role ever since.

Christian educators have taken these ideas and applied them to the church. in everything from how curriculum and books are written, to how children's classes are graded and structured, to what can children understand about God is affected. Bible related, kid-engaging activities such as crafts and games appear where only catechism instruction existed before.

"Every Church, Every Child" Curriculum

Methodist John Heyl Vincent and Baptist B. F. Jacobs took the Sunday School Movement to even greater heights of impact by establishing a "Uniform Lesson Plan" for Sunday Schools. Keith Drury, professor at Indiana Wesleyan University explains this plan: "As Sunday school developed thinkers saw the need for a more uniform plan of study that carefully covered the whole Bible in a set number of years, say eight. The incredible solution was the "Uniform Lesson plan" also called the "International Sunday school Lessons." This was a plan to have everybody of all ages in all denominations in the entire Christian world study the same passage of Scripture on the same Sunday. It worked!

Professor Keith Drury experienced this and wrote: "The idea spread so much that by 100 years ago virtually every Sunday school class of every denomination in the world studied the story of Jesus' temptation on the same day—every age in every denomination studying the same passage! This practice lasted well into the 1950s in many churches, including my own…when I was a kid the Presbyterian, Methodist, Baptist, and Wesleyan students in my high school all had the same Sunday school lesson last weekend. We could talk about our week's lesson at school like we'd been to the same church last Sunday. And, since virtually everyone had the same Bible lesson, people could tune in to the radio every week to hear "the lesson" taught by an expert. Indeed, many Sunday school teachers prepared by listening to these expert teachers teaching what would be an identical lesson in all churches."

Uniform Buildings

With Sunday School taking the same form throughout many denominations, the same building needs arose, too. Lewis Miller working with John Heyl Vincent and Jacob Snyder came up with the "Akron Plan" for Sunday School building layouts—a central assembly hall surrounded by small classrooms.

The Format Is Still Alive Today

The uniform lesson plan is still available in some denominations. Even among many of the new curriculum publishers today have chosen to echo elements of this format. Curriculums put out by Treasuring Christ and Gospel Project are two such publishers. They have chosen for everyone, from toddler to teen, to receive teaching on the same Bible passage every week. Many families and churches have found this approach helpful in guiding discussion in family worship times at home. However, this approach does have its drawbacks. It does not allow for teachers to target important topics relevant to certain ages; nor does it allow for different learning speeds within each age group. Really, it all comes down to knowing what will best help your church's particular families and children.

Pre-packaged Positives and Negatives

The expansion of children's ministry pre-packaged curriculum and Sunday School offerings during this period brought great good. Parents with very young children could worship, grow, and be equipped undistracted when basic, nursery care is provided. Children's classes can provide biblically sound teaching that supports the teaching parents give to their kids at home; while at the same time, providing an opportunity for special, adult classes. Children could be equipped with truths that could help them better connect with the preaching in the worship service. Educators who understand children better than the sweet, but untrained volunteer leading the class can write curriculum that helps these teachers teach well. These are good things.

The Gathering and Parental Responsibility Lost

However, not everything was good. Some theological moorings were lost during this Sunday School explosion. Among the most important set loose was the central importance of the worship gathering, even for children. Sunday School sometimes became a replacement for attending church, not just when the children are small and may not be able to understand or sit quietly, but all the way up into youth years. Sunday School becomes "Children's Church" which becomes "Youth Church" and the children coming to church completely miss church-- the very gathering of God's people that Sunday School was intended to prepare them for. Sunday School classes also began to be seen as the "professionals" parents relied upon to teach the Bible to their kids and even "see to it" that they were saved. They lost their sense of responsibility and opportunity to teach their children at home. These are terrible losses the church today is still trying to restore.

The Consumerized Church

For some, the church also became the place where you stop and shop for your own Bible knowledge and spiritual needs, instead of being God's people covenanting together to love the Lord and help equip one another to live the lives God has called them to live… including training up their kids. Perhaps these trends were not in the minds of the pioneers of the Sunday School movement, but they have certainly arisen with more prevalence, especially in the second half of the 20th century.

Slip in Theology

Another problem during this period was a change in theology in the boxed curriculum being published. Revivalism had passion, but that passion, over time, was not matched by depth in sound doctrine. Other pastors simply accepted the curriculum their denomination put out. They neglected to be the watchdog of sound doctrine they were supposed to provide for their flock.

CHILDREN'S MINISTRY IN CHURCH HISTORY

Lite, Not Light
Teaching often became lighter, to fit the new thoughts on what a child of a specific age could learn or would find interesting to learn. The original meaning of a Bible passage might be replaced with a simpler, often moralistic point instead. Exegesis is out, eisegesis to something more directly kid-friendly is in. On top of this, conversion often was conveyed as simply praying a simple prayer of faith, without the mention of repentance or discipleship.

Darkness Masquerading as Light
Even worse, the major liberal shifts in theology that occurred in the late 1800s oozed out into the curriculum of denominations like the Episcopal, Presbyterian, and Lutheran churches first, and later into the curriculum of the Methodists and even some of the Baptists during the 20th century. In some cases, the gospel was lost completely and remains lost even today. Thank God for the split in these denominations over these important, theological lines that occurred in the 1960s and 1970s and the sounder curriculum they produced that followed suit.

Tragically, many thousands of churches and millions of members still live in the darkness, unable to hold out anything but gospel-less moralism. How many good-hearted, well-intentioned godly men and women assume that if the materials they are using are printed and the church purchased it, then it must be good? Catechism-based teaching might have been increasingly considered "boring and unfriendly in style to children, but it was tethered closely to Scripture and God's purposes for His people.

Unreached Youth
While Sunday Schools were impacting the American children in the 1880s, Christian Endeavor was reaching out to youth and young adults.

Tied to the Church
Christian Endeavor was a church-based organization, originally started by Francis E. Clark, a minister in Portland, Maine. By the early 1900s there were over 67,000 "societies" around the world. The tone was intentional in these youth-led, adult-mentored chapters. "For Christ and the Church" was the motto.

Each Christian Endeavor participant made this vow: "Trusting in the Lord Jesus Christ for strength, I promise Him that I will strive to do whatever He would like to have me do; that I will make it the rule of my life to pray and to read the Bible every day, and to support the work and worship of my own church in every way possible; and that just so far as I know how, throughout my whole life, I will endeavor to lead a Christian life.

As an active member I promise to be true to all my duties, to be present at and to take some part, aside from singing, in every Christian Endeavor meeting, unless hindered by some reason which I can conscientiously give to my Lord and Master, Jesus Christ. If obliged to be absent from the monthly consecration meeting of the society, I will, if possible, send at least a verse of Scripture to be read in response to my name at the roll call."

Unlike many of the youth outreach organizations that would follow, Christian Endeavor was (and still is) dedicated to encouraging young people to gather with God's people at church, in keeping with the biblical model.

Impact Even Today on the Gospel

Much that is good and bad in children's ministry today has its foundation in new thinking and a new way of "doing" children's ministry from the Revivalism period. It is important to know how a child learns and teach in a way that they can understand. This is how pastors, parents, and teachers can employ what a child enjoys as a "conduit of truth" to make gospel truths something they can grasp and retain. But it this understanding discounts a child's ability to grasp biblical truths and replacing God's Word with only fun activities and morality, then the gospel is lost. We need to try to build on what is good for the sake of the gospel, not at the cost of the gospel.

The Church Needs True Conversion, Not Baptismal Statistics

Equally serious was the growing tendency to dilute the gospel. If teachers are handed curriculum that encourages the unhelpful "pray a simple prayer" variety of conversion, then immediately rings the "bell" of full assurance, this is not good. The urge for "conversions" is still sometimes rewarded with candy when a child prays a prayer today. Quotas for annual number of baptisms can become pressure for false conversions. Some churches have even taken to baptize children in entertaining ways that appeal to a child's sense of fun or an adult's approval, (such as a slide down a fire engine into the baptismal pool), instead of pointing to the seriousness of discipleship. This is no game. A number is no replacement for a life.

We absolutely want to regularly share the gospel with children and urge them to repent and believe in Christ. Many children do come to know the Lord from an early age. Praise God. But we need to give the children time to bear the fruit of conversion and discipleship that holds up under the test of time.

The Reactive Church (1920- present)

Reaction against Liberalism
What are you going to do about liberalism? Liberalism in theology and view of the Bible. Liberalism in the culture. Much of the past hundred years that has happened among Bible-believing Christians has been the answer to this question: "What are you going to do about the liberalism of theology?

The late 1880s brought a wave of criticism about the inerrancy of the Bible that affected first the seminaries through teaching, then flowed out into the mainline denominations, especially the Lutherans, Presbyterians, Episcopalians and the Northern Baptists. By the 1920s, the teaching from the pulpits as well as the curriculum produced by their publishing houses would have lost much of the gospel. Some reacted by separating themselves completely—such as those who would be called "fundamentalists" and those who would come out from their denominations to form new, conservative ones, such as the PCA.

The Gospel and Shunned Culture
The fundamentalists would also decide to separate themselves more fully from the culture, too. Homeschooling was popular within these circles decades before it grew wider following in the 1970's To support that movement came publishers like Bob Jones to help families educate their children.

They made stricter lifestyle changes apart of their membership requirements (women wearing pants/men with long hair/dancing and drinking, etc.), choice of Bible translation (KJV), as well as upholding to inerrancy of the Bible. Preaching from the pulpit, teaching from Sunday Schools and life at home would have included teaching along both these cultural lines and biblical lines. It would be hard to distinguish between the two in children's minds. The atmosphere for disagreement was restrictive. To disagree would be to separate. It would feel like ostracism. This added temptation to fake Christianity and sneak in rebellion in order to remain in community. This tendency still exists today.

The Gospel and Culture Connection
Neo-evangelicals became the name of those who separated themselves from the liberal denominations but wanted to stay engaged with the American culture. They saw themselves as custodians of biblical Christianity in America (and in Britain), and wanted to push back against liberalism reach and claims against the Bible. Some of these rose up as independent, non-denominational churches, some as new denominations, such as the PCA. New Bible schools and seminaries were established filled with bright, conservative scholars who fought back in their classes and through their commentaries. New finds in archaeology (such as the Dead Sea Scrolls) would only act to affirm these scholar's stance to trust the Bible. These new institutions would train up and feed a new generation of preachers to feed Bible truths to congregations once more. New preaching in these churches would provide families with Bible truths to equip themselves and their children. Some would be expositional. But most of the evangelical churches would be a bit lighter, more topical, in keeping with a desire to "reach people where they were."

Parachurch Paramedics
Many parachurch organizations sprung up to support these evangelicals who previously received such support from their denominations. Gospel Light, David C. Cook, and Moody were the first supports in the curriculum world. Many others have followed in the decades since. These materials provided the biblically-based curriculum no longer being printed in the publishing houses of the mainline denominations. That was good. But, in a desire to stay in business and to please many from different denominations, a happy medium of truth would have to be chosen.

Non-denominational publishing houses were only the tip of the parachurch iceberg. Parachurch ministries mushroomed. Everything from Focus on the Family on the radio, to AWANAs for kids, Campus Crusade and Inter-Varsity Christian Fellowship on the college campuses, World Vision and Compassion International in mercy ministries, TEAM and YWAM in missions. Each had its own statement of faith holding to basic, biblical truths that all evangelicals accepted and leaving out distinctives of differing denominations in order to be acceptable to all. These organizations provided an infrastructure that served the many evangelical churches who no longer had a denominational, biblically conservative anchor.

Some of the services they provided have borne great fruit and have been a huge help. Unfortunately, their lack of church affiliation meant less emphasis on the importance of membership in a church. College students might simply attend their campus meetings and consider themselves well-fed. Their leaders too frequently did not encourage church attendance, setting their students up for simply leaving off church when they graduated from college, no longer able to find the same "homogenous" fellowship they enjoyed. No wonder many of these students would later be attracted to churches offering niche services to meet their particular needs, instead of a body of believers focused on each other through a strong membership model.

Gospel In-Culturated
This trend to meet people where they are was taken to an explosive, new level with the Church Growth movement. The Church Growth movement during this period sought to build church campuses to attract non-Christians with culturally friendliness. Daycare, gyms, baseball fields, dance classes, coffee shops on site. Video clips, big worship bands, darkened auditoriums that promote anonymity and a concert feel, seeker friendly "keep it gospel light" services. These are some of the strategies used to bring in those not used to church and keep them coming back.

The children's and youth programs are built to please, too. Prolific, entertaining, and custom-built for each age. Children's Church. Youth Church. College Church. But rarely the whole church gathered together. Growth comes and the mega-church is born. Multi-site, multi-service. Enough for everyone, but it is hard to get to know much of anyone. The intention is to create a comfortable atmosphere in which to share the gospel that many might be saved. But how hard will it be in this model for the aroma of the gospel in the air to be strong enough to be noticed as a distinct smell?

Parents may join small groups or get connected in interest groups on campus and find accountability and encouragement in raising their children in this way, but it takes extra effort to not melt into anonymity. Big-budget programs can support great curriculum that reaches the hearts of children in an understanding, enjoyable, and memorable way, but too much entertainment can actually be distracting to the very gospel it hopes to communicate. And seeker-friendly services with simple sermons may be easy for a newcomer to swallow, but how much food do they offer God's people to live and grow from? What do they have to give their kids? Membership is too often seen as unwelcoming instead of a covenant made in a community of love who wants to help you grow in godliness.

Gospel Plus Experience
The rise of Pentecostalism and the teaching of the need for signs and wonders and a post-conversion second filling of the Holy Spirit has been another very significant influence during the last 100 years. Growing out of the Azuza Street Revival in 1906, came the Holiness and Assemblies of God churches as well as many other independent churches. Others have continued this tradition down to today. They see themselves as the modern Apostolic Church. Experience, not preaching, tends to be "king" in these churches. Christians are expected to speak in tongues as a sign of conversion. Preaching is skewed by this interpretation and has a great impact upon who is considered a Christian, difficult both for parents

and for children.

Gospel through the Family
Some reacted to the growing world and church culture by focusing on family-centered training. By 1970s the homeschool movement was more than just a fringe movement of the fundamentalists and a few other groups. More and more Christian families wanted to have more time with their kids before sending them out into the world. Abeka and Bob Jones publishing houses had to make way for dozens of new curriculum providers. As the culture continues to shift, this trend has only increased. This has not only given many families control over their children's general education needs, but their spiritual ones as well. Many of these curriculums are Christian-based and include Bible teaching. Parents have more resources that ever to diligently train up their children. Sunday School curriuclum even transfers over to use in home school, blending teaching at church with teaching in the home.

Gospel Minus Congregation
Advocates of the Family-integrated movement have taken parental responsibility for their children's spiritual training one radical step further. These parents believe that they alone are to be their children's teachers. Children do not attend Sunday School or any other classes. They only are to go to church with their parents. I admire the seriousness with which these parents take their God-given responsibility. And, I love the primacy they place on the preaching of God's Word to feed God's people gathered. However, I feel they miss the point that the church is made up of fellow encouragers in the faith. We are made to help equip each other. For some families, the support the church can supply helps them better fulfill what God calls them to do as parents. This model does not allow such families to get that help.

Biblical Gospel Gatherings
Over the years, as the evangelical church has increasingly lost its taste for a depth of theology and/or a confidence that children and families need or want it, it has become increasingly shallow. This did not go unnoticed or unaddressed. Enter the reformation resurgence.

Remember the Reformation
During this same time period, 1920s to the present, there have been those whose reaction to liberalism has been to look back, learn and restore the biblical model of expositional preaching, sound doctrine, and strong church membership. They looked first of all to the biblical model, but also to the best practices of it through the ages, giving lots of attention to the churches of the reformation. Arminianism as well as liberalism; revivalism as well as Pentecostalism; rejecting the culture and playing too much to the culture, left the church indistinct and unhealthy. These men wanted to bring back the witness and the health of the church.

In my husband's talk, "Where Did All These Calvinists Come From?" my husband mentions the parade of men, organizations, and movements as important in this ideology: J. Gresham Machen, Charles Spurgeon, Martyn Lloyd-Jones, Banner of Truth Trust, Evangelism Explosion, Carl Henry, PCA, J.I. Packer, John MacArthur and R.C. Sproul, John Piper, Reformed Rap, influential parachurch ministries (such as Southern Baptist Theological Seminary and Nine Marks). Churches like Sovereign Grace have even had an impact on those previously of a Pentecostal bent. These have had a strong impact in their local churches, through their preaching and speaking, and even more broadly, through the books printed or materials made available online.

Impact on Children and Families
In addition to Banner of Truth, publishers like Crossway, Christian Focus and Children Desiring God have provided many biblically-rich resources for families to use at home or as curriculum at church. The

renewed use of traditional catechisms as well as creation of new ones, (and these not just in written form but set to music and in apps as well) has helped many families fill their children with a strong legacy of deep truths to last them a lifetime.

Healthy Churches
The return to expositional preaching has provided the nutritious teaching that equips families with what they need to train up their children at home, through their own witness as well as teaching them Bible truths. Strengthened members make better encouragers and nurturers of each other as well as teachers of the children in Bible classes. A careful membership process makes true conversion clearer and the witness of the congregation more Christ-like. Discipline promotes the daily repentance, dependence on God's grace and call to discipleship believers need. Children are treated with respect and their response to the gospel treated with watchful waiting, knowing that they need time to mature before coming into membership, for the sake of their assurance of faith and the witness of the church.

No surprise here, given who I'm married to, that I've seen the good fruit of this particular trend in my lifetime.

Children's Ministry Lessons from Church History

As goes the church, so goes the family and children's ministry. Church history in the 2000+ year old testimony to the biblical model being the best model for the health of the church, present and future.

#1 The Blessing of the Biblical Model
When the Bible is clearly preached, God is worshiped, and discipleship is taught and lived out, the soil is rich for God's Holy Spirit to bring the gift of repentance and faith to the next generation. History bears witness to this.

#2: Harm Where We Go Astray
But, when the Word is maligned, or misused to teach false doctrine, or withheld from the church, the church and its families suffer. When worship of God is replaced with the worship of saints or tradition or popes or false prophets, the church and its families suffer. When the witness of the church is obscured by false conversion, lack of discipleship, undisciplined membership, anonymity, and lack of care between members, the church and its families suffer.

#3: Don't Stop Fighting the Good Fight
This is why contending for the faith is the constant work of the church. Every period of church history tends towards different issues in one or more of these areas, showing up as struggles or weaknesses affecting the whole church, including parents and children.

#4 Children's Ministry Helps Most When It Supports (Not Supplants) the Gathering of God's People and Children with Them
Children's ministry can be as simple as God's people being fed in the weekly gatherings of the local church for the equipping of parents to train their children at home. Many times, it includes programs in addition to this. At its best, children's ministry always keeps the gathering of the local church in mind and provides support that complements it. At its worst, children's ministry is used to create a separate track for children that carries into youth and even college. There is little opportunity to understand what the church is supposed to be.

#5 Take Care with Baptizing Children
Baptism of children upon their walking down an aisle or praying a simple prayer too often leads to false sense of assurance and hurts the witness of the church. Waiting for the fruit of conversion that comes with maturity is best for all.

#6 Only by the Grace of God
Despite the sinfulness and wanderings of His people, God has and always will be faithful to preserve a remnant of people for Himself. His plans will always succeed and His whole church will be brought in. But if God's people know nothing else that Day as stand there before His throne, it is that they only stand in His presence by His grace, power, and forgiveness. None of them--none of us-- are worthy, but by the blood of the Lamb that covers us. None is faithful, but by the power of His Holy Spirit, for the glory of His name.

Section 4
Where Are We Today?

Children's Ministry Today
The goals of those 1870s Sunday Schools remain largely the same today, though some, like the importance of gathering together with the whole church body, may have retreated to the background or at least not not be as clearly articulated. Churches still invite children from non-Christian families to take part in their programs. They still hold out the gospel to all, that they might be saved and grow as Christ's disciples. They still hope to leave a legacy of Bible truths in their minds and heart.

But now, in most churches, Children's Ministry often spends far more time on programs and resources for Christian parents and children (perhaps this is because they are spending less time on outreach to children). And most notably of all, most churches have expanded to many more programs than the original Sunday School Bible classes and church attendance. Now, they frequently include safe nursery-care for babies, so parents can go to their own Sunday School classes. They may be recommending resources for parents to use at home with their children; and, they may have added a host of other, now-classic, peripheral programs (such as youth group, children's choir, AWANAs, After school Good News Clubs, Mother's Day Out, Sunday night missions programs, Bible camps, Vacation Bible School, and even Children or Youth Church that caters to a particular, homogenous age group.)

All of This Growth Has Led to Mixed Results
These intentions, and even some of the fruit, of these increased programs of today's typical Children's Ministry, has been good. But sometimes the burgeoning list of programs has led to serious fallout for parents, children, and the volunteers who people these activities. The motto of "If you make the children happy, then the parents will stay" might bring more families to church, but it can unintentionally lead to malnutrition. Parents can begin to lose their sense of calling as primary, spiritual caregivers, or at least struggle to find time to fulfill it. Children may become so used to being catered for in a custom-fit, homogenous-group style that they lose their taste for the more important influences of family time and/or gathering together to worship with the whole church body. Overused volunteers may struggle with burnout and suffer from neglect of their own spiritual nourishment at church.

More at Any Cost?
"More is not just better, but necessary" is the even uglier step-sister motto that frequently accompanies the "If you make the children happy, the families will stay" motto. This line of reasoning exacerbates the problems mentioned above, in every size of church.

Small, churches and church plants frequently face the frustrations of not having enough man-power to keep open the children's programs that visiting families are seeking. Or, even if they do manage to have all the "wish list" programs in place, they often tend to rely too heavily on too few volunteers. These tireless, big-hearted servants often sacrifice their own spiritual needs, week after week, to make sure the children's programs stay running.

Medium and large churches face their own version of these same problems. As the number of children and volunteers expands, the tendency is for churches to expand their program offerings, instead of first seeking healthier volunteer service limits with the programs they have. This plethora of programs can perpetuate the volunteer crisis. Yes, there are more able volunteers, but now so many more are needed to maintain the large number of programs.

Churches with more pocket money than volunteers find a solution by hiring caregivers who aren't members of their church. Others are tempted to enlist people who aren't really qualified to teach, choose a curriculum because it's an easy fit, even though it lacks biblical soundness; or, "fudge" on safe caregiver-to-child ratios to fit in more children.

And, if parents are not urged to be discerning, their children's schedules may so fill up with programs that the very families you hoped to serve with all these activities, can't find time to just be a family.

Pastors may be so overwhelmed with other aspects of ministry that they leave oversight of these matters in the hands of others who should be helpers, rather than shepherds over this segment of their church's growth.

Enter Church-Shaped Children's Ministry

Church-shaped Children's Ministry is a humble, finite approach to caring well for the families within the context of a healthy church. It acknowledges parents in their role as primary spiritual caregivers of their children and it encourages them in ways that are in keeping with the spiritual well-being of all of its members. It looks to its pastors to set priorities for the spiritual support of parents and children; and, to carefully assess what resources (volunteers, finances, facility space, hours, etc.) the church has to offer towards those priorities. They prayerfully consider the best fit for the good of the whole church, and to the glory of God. Then, they lead the members in carrying it out.

More about Church-Shaped Children's Ministry?

Want to know more about Church-Shaped Children's Ministry? The next two appendices provide a lot more information.

Visit the Praise Factory website for lots more free resources. Particularly, you might want to look at the Church-shaped Children's Ministry Workshop book and the Praise Factory Pitchbook. Also, Build on Jesus, by Deepak Reju and Marty Machiowski has some wonder chapters regarding these ideas. Published by New Growth Press. Available on Amazon.

APPENDIX D

Church-Shaped Children's Ministry: Mindful of the Gatherings

Church-Shaped Children's Ministry Overview

Church-Shaped Children's Ministry Is Mindful of the Gatherings

- It points to the gathering of God's people, in heaven at the end of time and on earth, every Sunday.

- It is organized so that everything else that happens in children's ministry is a support to this basic model that the pastors lead their local church in providing to help families.

- It wants this support to be helpful in leading everyone to taking part in the gatherings: parents, children, member volunteers, and children's ministry leaders.

- Is an outflow of the church's covenant to aid each other in growing in maturity in Christ and in living out in godliness the good works God has planned for their lives.

Church-Shaped Children's Ministry Is Lead by the Pastors/Elders

- Who feed parents and children from the pulpit.

- Who decide what programs the church offers parents and children.

- Who make sure children's ministry echoes the teaching priorities of the church.

- Who make sure children's ministry reflects the resources of the church (financial, facilities, spiritually-healthy serve limits for volunteers).

- Who keep the people involved in children's ministry (families, children, volunteers, staff) under their guidance and care.

- Who make children's ministry a path towards all gathering to worship together.

Church-Shaped Children's Ministry Supports, Not Supplants Parents

- It acknowledges that parents are called by God to be the primary, spiritual caregivers of their children.

- It also understands that parents are not Christians, alone, but are members of the local church, who encourage and build one another up, including encouraging and helping each other to spiritually nurture their children well.

Church-Shaped Children's Ministry Desires to Train Children

- To provide children with a faithful testimony of life with God in the lives of their parents, teachers, and other members.

- To share the gospel with children that the lost might be saved.

- To make disciples of all children who trust in Christ.

- To leave a legacy of Bible truths and knowledge of Scripture in the minds of the children.

- To prepare children to gather together well with the members of a local church.

Church-Shaped Children's Ministry Is Rooted in the Worship Gathering

- It recognizes the basic biblical model of children's ministry for families to be equipped through preaching, strengthened by worship, and encouraged by fellow members at church to carry on training up their children in the nurture and admonition of the Lord at home.

- It sees itself as an aid to help children to gather together meaningfully with God's people and Lord willing, as God's people.

Church-Shaped Children's Ministry Often Includes Other Programs

- That partner with the preaching.

- That help prepare the children to gather together well with the congregation.

- That are sustainable, in terms of finances and volunteers required.

- That support, not replace, parents.

- That don't get in the way with family time.

Church-Shaped Children's Ministry Enlists Fellow Church Members

- To help equip each other in caring well for their children, at home and at church.

- To prepare them to be, Lord willing, future members of the church.

Church-Shaped Children's Ministry Is Rooted in the Worship Gathering

- They work under the leadership of the pastors and are cared for through their leadership.

- They bring the pastoral vision to life through curriculum, volunteers, and generally encouraging families.

**SO THAT... all might gather together,
for the good of the whole church, and to the glory of God.**

Section 2
Church-Shaped Children's Ministry
Is Mindful of the Gatherings

If you know about Nine Marks ministries, you know that it encourages "building healthy churches". (And if you don't know about it, you should go take a look at 9marks.org. It will make a lot more sense of what I'm going to tell you.) Church-shaped children's ministry, as well as all the other Praise Factory resources is Nine Mark's little sister. First of all, because it also has grown up in the Capitol Hill Baptist Church family and it has been my labor of love alongside my husband, Mark Dever, as he has pastored this church. But most of all, because it is the scribe of how we have seen those Nine Marks have made a huge difference in children's ministry at CHBC and many other churches around the world. They really have helped our pastors keep children's ministry "Church-shaped," that is, to keep the gathering of God's people the main thing behind everything we do in children's ministry.

Hebrews 10:22-25 goes a long way in describing church-shaped children's ministry:
"…let us draw near to God with a sincere heart and with the full assurance that faith brings, having our hearts sprinkled to cleanse us from a guilty conscience and having our bodies washed with pure water. Let us hold unswervingly to the hope we profess, for he who promised is faithful. And let us consider how we may spur one another on toward love and good deeds, not giving up meeting together, as some are in the habit of doing, but encouraging one another—and all the more as you see the Day approaching."

Let's take a look at how everything in Church-shaped Children's Ministry points not only to the Great Gathering at the end of time, but to the gatherings here on earth that prepare God's people for that Day.

Church-Shaped Children's Ministry
Points to the Gatherings

1. Points to the Great Gathering of God with all of His people.
What happens on that "Day" that verse 25 mentions? Two main things. Those who rejected God's offer of salvation through Jesus will go to their final punishment for sins. They did not draw near to God and now they will never get that opportunity. Their hearts were not cleansed from their guilty conscience. They did not trust in Christ. They were not buried with His death, nor raised to life with Him (vs. 22). They have no hope. Only judgement. Oh, so very sad!

But for those who did repent of their sins and trust in Christ as their only Savior, this will be the Day of the Great Gathering of all of God's people with God forever. A day to enjoy the Feast of the Lamb with the Lamb: "Then I heard what sounded like a great multitude, like the roar of rushing waters and like loud peals of thunder, shouting: "Hallelujah! For our Lord God Almighty reigns. Let us rejoice and be glad and give him glory! For the wedding of the Lamb has come, and his bride has made herself ready. Fine linen, bright and clean, was given her to wear." --Revelation 19:6-8

This is the great Day that God's people yearn for and that all of history points to. This is where the Church at last really looks like a bride, without blemish. This is where she really acts like a bride, full of love for her groom. It is also the Day when those who refused to repent and believe in Jesus as their Savior will go to their final punishment. No one is left unaffected by this Day.

First and foremost, Church-Shaped Children's Ministry points to this gathering. That's why we want to prepare everyone for it.

This means clearly teaching them the gospel; and, clearly explaining what it means to be a disciple --one who turns away from their old way of life and turns and trust and obedience to Christ. AND, teaching them to commit themselves to a local gathering of the church for guidance under godly pastors, instruction in God's Word, the worship of God, and the care and encouragement of one another. the good news of salvation to children that they, too, might be a part of that Great Gathering of God's people.

2. Points to the earthly gathering of local churches each week.
And that's why church-shaped children's ministry also points to those regular, earthly gatherings of God's people in the local church each week. If the Great Gathering of God's people with God is the grand finale, the gathering of God's people in the local church is the weekly dress rehearsal. We are to gather regularly—not give up meeting together. We are to spur one another one to love and good deeds—through the preaching of God's Word, through our corporate worship, and through us loving and encouraging one another (vs.25).

Families are to be a part of these gatherings. Children watch and learn as they are part of the gatherings. They hear God's Word. They watch God's people worship Him. They witness God's people loving each other and enjoy that love, themselves. And Lord willing, faith will come by hearing and hearing by the Word of Christ. (Romans 10:17, ESV) and they will join with God's people, and as God's people, in worship and witness, too.

These gatherings are crucial for parents, too. Parents are equipped through the preaching of God's Word, they are strengthened through the worship of God, and they are helped by each other, encouraged by wisdom, sharing, praying, serving, teaching, and admonishing to live godly lives. Lives that can be a powerful witness to their children. Through the church, parents are equipped for all of life and godliness—including for their job as primary spiritual caregivers (disciplers) of their children, both in the pew and at home.

Church-shaped Children's Ministry also means being mindful of those who care for the children to be ready for that Day, too. It seeks to care for the one (families), without neglecting the other (member volunteers) through the regular gathering of God's people at church (vs.25). Being too busy serving the children and missing these gatherings is another way of neglecting to gather together (Hebrews 10:25)

3. Even points to the family gatherings of godly parents with their children at home.
The minutes families spend each week in the church pale in comparison to the days they spend together each week at home. If the grand finale is the heavenly, Great Gathering of all God's people, and the weekly gatherings of the local church are the dress rehearsals, then home life is the daily "play practice" gatherings as godly parents carry on "training up their children in the nurture and admonition in the Lord" through their life's witness, through their daily worship of the Lord, and the instruction from God's Word they give them. (Deuteronomy 6:7, 11:19; Ephesians 6:1-4)

Where do families, particularly parents, get their "lines" to speak out into their lives and their children's lives, Monday through Saturday? Through their own time in pray and in God's Word at home during the week, no doubt. But, even more so, on Sundays, when they gather together with God's people.

This leads us to the very core of children's ministry: providing for families THROUGH the weekly, worship gathering, itself.

Church-Shaped Children's Ministry Provides Through the Worship Gathering at Church

The most basic, biblical model of children's ministry is to provide for families through the gathering of the local church of believers. This comes through worshipping God together, through sitting under the preaching of God's Word, and by receiving encouragement and aid from fellow members who work to present each other mature in Christ (Colossians 1:28). We are to spur one another on towards love and good works (Hebrews 10:25), including the good work of helping each other raise the children under our care.

The worship gathering is not just about equipping parents for the training of their children. It is to be a place where children see God's people worship, hear God's Word preached, and watch God's people display God in how they love one another. And Lord willing, as they see, hear and watch, the Lord will work in their hearts, bringing them to repent and believe in Him, themselves.

But how can we strategically and make the most of the worship gathering to help parents and children?

Ways to Provide through the Gathering:

The Service

- Provide a simple worship bulletin and pencils/crayons for kids. This can be an especially customized worship bulletin for each particular service; or, check out Truth78's spiral-bound service "templates" that can be used with any service. Great for use in the service. Great for parents to use with their children at home to review what they learn.

- Provide blank paper and pencils/crayons for the kids and ask them to draw a picture of something from the service and give it to the pastor at the end of the service. One pastor told me he takes these pictures and posts them on his office door. The kids love this.

- Give away books/make book suggestions that would be helpful to parents or their children to use at home.

- Adding a catechism question (one of your own making or from a simple, kids catechism) to the service or at least in the bulletin that fits in with the theme of the service.

- Include children and their families in the worship service prayers.

- A few pastors/worship service leaders I spoke to told me they especially welcome the youngest children (usually 4/5year olds) to the service during the opening welcome time. They would ask these children to raise their hands to show him where they were seated. Apparently, this has been a huge encouragement to these children and has helped them to want to pay attention in the service.

The Songs

- Provide mp3 links (such as on your church's website) to hymns and other sons you sing in your gatherings for families to listen to and learn at home.

- Include the words and music to the songs in printed bulletins for them to take home and use in family worship times.

- Be intentional with your service music. Choose songs in advance and let the congregation know what you will be singing. This is especially good for introducing new songs. At CHBC, new songs are introduced, then sung three weeks in a row in our preparation music time on Sunday mornings. This is singing that takes place during the 15 minutes leading up to the official start of the service. It's a great way to learn new songs.

- The church also informs the congregation about new songs being introduced in the weekly e-newsletter that goes out on Wednesdays. It includes links to the new songs for them to listen to and learn from.

- Introducing songs in the service by providing a simple explanation of some of the "big, Bible words" in the lyrics. You can do this verbally as you introduce the song or even include it in the bulletin.

The Fellowship

- Include a section in the back of your membership directory of families including names of children. Encourage your members to pray for the families as they pray through the directory (Our church has been training to regularly pray through the directory and this has been a great way to learn the names of children and to ask God's blessings upon them.)

- Encourage the congregation to ask intentional questions and share vulnerably so they can truly give each other godly encouragement and advice that builds up. Take time to pray for each other as you share. Parenting can be so hard. Advice from others, especially those who have children older than yours can be so helpful. Grace from our prayer-answering God can be even more helpful!

- Encourage husbands, wives, couples, etc. getting together to talk and pray about family matters—everything from discipline to discipleship.

- Encourage families to adopt singles or couples without children into their lives. Families can provide a natural training ground for these future parents. And, these singles/couples can be yet another reflection of Christ to the children, as well as help for the parents.

The Sermon

- Teach parents about their calling as primary disciplers of their children.

- Print a sermon card (or make available on your website) upcoming sermons and Scripture passages. Families can read these passages in the week leading up to your sermon. Some families even try to come up with a 3-point outline or at least keywords that will be emphasized in the sermon. After the sermon, they discuss how close they were.

- Use a simple, outline format that will help even young children follow along; and, can be used by families at home, if they have a "sermon review" time during lunch.

- Think about the basic pitch of your sermon (one pastor friend told me he always pitched his sermon to a bright 16-year-old.)

- Choose illustrations that even they can understand.

- Choose a few, key concepts, such as gospel, disciple, grace, faith, and repent to regularly explain in very simple terms when preaching.

- Regularly include ways members can encourage parents and children through conversation and acts of service.

- Give the children a question to ask their parents when they go home (such as "Ask your parents about a time they struggled with fear and God helped them.")

- Post sermons online for parents to listen to another time if noisy children kept them from absorbing the content during the service. Or, to even be able to use portions with their children to lead discussions at home (with older children/youth).

Some Helpful Resources

- Parenting in the Pew: Guiding Your Children in the Joy of Worship   Robbie Castleman

- Truth:78 Resources, such as "My Church Notebook" and "Children and the Worship Service" by David and Sally Michael

- Build on Jesus Marty Machiowski and Deepak Reju

CHURCH-SHAPED CHILDREN'S MINISTRY PROVIDES THROUGH THE WORSHIP GATHERING AT CHURCH

Because Scripture points to the centrality of these gatherings, children's ministry needs to, too.

It starts here, with this basic, biblical model:

**In light of the Day to come,
The Church gathers, led by pastors:**

- **Word:** To instruct and equip God's people for life and godliness, including parenting

- **Worship:** Strengthened and growing as they worship God and meditate on His character.

- **Witness:** Seeking to actively build one another in the faith, seeking to present everyone mature in Christ, by prayer and acts of love, by encouragement and reproof; by teaching and example; seeing that you are in the faith and continuing in the faith. By God's grace, being an increasing witness to all of Christ, including the children in their midst. (2 Corinthians 3:18)

**In light of each week to come:
Families continue the training at home, led by parents:**

- **Word:** Equipped at church, they continue to instruct their children in God's Word at home.

- **Worship:** Strengthened at church, they continue to worship the Lord at home, before their children and with their children, if they come to faith, themselves.

- **Witness:** Continuing the reflection of Christ at home in how they discipline and love their children. and before them, live their lives in love to God.

Lord willing, the Holy Spirit uses the gatherings at church as well as the training at home in the hearts of the children. He works in their hearts, helping them to repent, believe, and become Jesus' disciples and fellow church members themselves one day. Short. Sweet. Basic.

THIS IS THE BASIC CHILDREN'S MINISTRY MODEL

**In a very real sense,
if you are faithful in this basic, biblical model mentioned above,
you are being faithful in Children's Ministry,
to parents and children.**

Beyond Basic

But usually, children's ministry winds up including a lot more than this basic, biblical model. Many churches provide childcare, Sunday School, and many other programs for children. They also often provide extra teaching times for adults. These can be great services that help parents and children grow in their knowledge of God.

But this is also when things get complicated, many times unhealthily complicated. Time at church, which should be pointing to the gathering of God's people, winds up losing its direction. The main thing no longer seems to be the main thing.

**The next sections are dedicated to thinking about how you might add more
while still keeping the gathering the main thing.**

BEYOND BASIC
Church-Shaped Children's Ministry Provides for the Worship Gathering at Church

When thinking about going beyond the basic, biblical model, start with providing FOR the gathering. That is, what parents/children would especially benefit from extra help so they can be better equipped through the worship service themselves?

Often, providing for the worship gathering includes programs like these:

1. Safe childcare (no teaching) for infants and toddlers during the worship service

These little people are obviously limited in their ability to understand what's going on in the service, but not limited in their ability to disrupt the service. Providing something as basic as childcare so that parents can focus on the service may sound just like babysitting on Tuesday night, and in some ways, it may look like it. But encourage your volunteers that it is not! They are supporting the preaching of the Word and the building up of the congregation through their service. It's like turning up the volume of the hearing aid of someone with a hearing deficit. They are playing an important role in equipping parents to teach their children at home. That's a big deal with even eternal consequences.

Note: Don't provide child care for anyone but your own children unless you have a child-protection policy in place.

Helpful Resources:
On Guard Deepak Reju
Safe Kids: Policies and Procedures for Keeping Kids Safe in Church

2. Providing teaching during all/part of the worship service for younger children that phases out as they get older

If church-shaped children's ministry emphasizes the importance of the worship gatherings for families, why would it ever include programs during part or, even more radical, all of a service? Isn't this a contradiction? It certainly could be. Some churches provide programs that start with newborns and continue all the way up through high school and even college! This "stovepipe" shape that never brings children into the full gathering is a terrible idea, no doubt coming from the well-intentioned "give them what they like and they will keep coming back" mentality. But this approach assumes the smell of "custom-made kid-liness" in these homogenous "services" is better than the not-as-familiar, aroma of Christ and the gospel that waifs out of the whole-church worship services. Church-shaped Children's Ministry is definitely NOT advocating this kind of approach.

But it doesn't necessarily mean you never offer any children classes during all or part of the service. It does mean that you gradually add them in as they mature. For example, if you have really long sermons (like we do here at CHBC) you might provide, something for preschoolers during the whole service and even something for younger elementary-school age children for the sermon portion of the service. We have chosen to offer two such classes. Preschoolers have their own meaty class during the entire service that parents may choose to put their children in. Our younger elementary-school age kids are included in the first 45 minutes of singing, prayers and Bible reading, but can be excused during the sermon portion of the service to their own teaching time.

CHURCH-SHAPED CHILDREN'S MINISTRY PROVIDES FOR THE WORSHIP GATHERING AT CHURCH

This is where we use the Praise Factory curriculum for both the preschoolers and young elementary-school age kids. The curriculum includes elements like what the children experience in the worship service, including prayers, Bible reading, and a story sermon with listening questions that help prepare them for purposeful listening, like they will do in the worship service.

Even though these children are missing all or part of the service for a few years, what we have chosen to do helps them prepare for the gathering for many more years to come. And, we are always encouraging the parents to pull their kids out and bring them I mean to keep their kids in for the sermon and see how they do. As they see a continued pattern of readiness, they may have the kids go out less frequently. And even though we offer Praise Factory for those older kids through third grade, we very frequently have parents who are pulling their kids out to sit with them all the time to the sermon earlier than that. The curriculum also provides a meaty take-home bulletin That includes the him they're learning the scripture their learning the story they're learning and ACTS prayer (Adoration, Confession, Thanksgiving, Supplication) that they're learning so that parents can continue to prepare their kids to gather together with the gathering even in their home devotion times.

And, for as many parents who do include their children in any of the "ramp-up to worship" classes we provide during the worship service, there are many who choose to keep their children with them. The elders have served the whole congregation well by encouraging an attitude of respect for these differences of opinion. Many churches have not fared so well, having been rattling with parents who firmly feel that their view on these matters is the only "biblical" view. Many well-meaning family-integrated families have sadly been implicated here. Pastors, preach to your congregation the importance of unity in gospel essentials, but Christian freedom in how families, in good conscience, use the members of the church family to help equip the members of their own family.

Church-Shaped Children's Ministry Provides for the Gathering at Home

In addition to equipping parents and training children through the worship service, churches may have a library, book stall, or provide a book list of helpful books for parents to use with their children. Often, take-home sheets are provided with Sunday School curriculum. In my experience, I've found that two issues frequently keep good books out of the needy hands of families. One: parents who are very busy. and don't get around to getting books. And two: most of the best books are only available online, making it even harder for busy parents to find time to search for books, make sure they are good fit for their children, and actually use them. For this reason, we actually do all three of the above things, plus a few more:

1. Annual Bookfair
We host a once-a-year book fair in November (in time for the holidays) on a Saturday/Sunday at church. We have done this as a "Look Only" book fair as well as a "Buy What's There" Book Fair. We include a comprehensive list of all the books on hand as well as articles to help parents think through catechisms, Bible story books, Bibles and other related topics. This annual list goes up on our website for families to continue to access throughout the year.

This has been a big hit for parents getting their hands on resources and finding what's just right for their family and children. Perhaps of as much value has been the conversations we have with the parents. It's a real "pastoral" event in that we learn so much more about the individual challenges and struggles particular families are facing. Information that helps us serve them better in other ways.

Note: Visit the Capitol Hill Baptist Church website and you can view or download the hefty 40+page booklist we have compiled. We try to update this list once a year.

2. Pulpit Give-aways
Our pastors give away books every week from the pulpit, including books for parents or children. This gives them a chance to tell the congregation about books they particularly like and why. This helps not only the lucky parent who gets the free hand-out, but everyone else who hears about it. We've had members still asking months later about one or other book a pastor recommended and gave away; as well as stories of how the one parent who received the free book went on to share the resource with others.

3. Curriculum with Take Homes and Online Access
We use curriculum with beefy take-home sheets and online access to the full curriculum for use with parents. While some parents may not choose to use these, we find that some do.

4. Quarterly Newsletters and Bi-monthly Members' Meetings
We always try to include reviews of a few books in the newsletters and at members' meetings that would be useful to parents with their families.

Church-Shaped Children's Ministry Prepares for the Worship Gathering at Church

Many churches provide classes for children and adults, in addition to the preaching of God's Word in the worship service. The great thing about having a separate Sunday School hour is that it does not interfere with teachers or families taking part in the worship service. They also can provide focused, age-appropriate instruction in Bible truths that helps both child and parent to get more out of the worship service.

Let's take a look at some variations of this two-hundred-year classic, first for children, then for adults.

Sunday School Hour: Preparing the Children

The good and bad news is that there is a ton of curriculum options for Sunday School. It takes discernment to weed through the bad theology found in some of these options. A willingness to make adjustments to fit your teachers and children, even from the best the market has to offer. But put in the effort and you leave a rich legacy. Here are four types of "curriculum" frequently used.

1. Simple catechism and/or Bible memory time

There are some GREAT catechism and Bible verse materials that even set the questions and answers to music. I particularly like New City Catechism and the Truth 78 Fighter verses. Both are set to music. The New City Cathechism even includes a devotional guide you can use in class or recommend to parents to use at home with their children. There are multiple levels of difficulty available for both of these resources. In addition, now there are Fighter Verse coloring books that can be used. One warning: be careful to not discourage kids who do not memorize easily. Sometimes those stinking star charts on display are so hard for kids like this! Make the point the meaning of the verses or catechism answer, not the perfection of the words. I know many children who cringed to go to classes because they felt like losers at Bible memory. Memory is partially a skill. Understanding is the goal that God will use to change hearts. Keep your eyes on that prize.

2. "Teach from the Worship Bulletin" classes

Teachers can use the actual worship service framework to help children think about what they will learn in the service. This can include singing the songs, reading and thinking about the Bible verses, and leading in prayer. Many times, services will focus on a particular attribute of God and all of the prayers and songs flow out of that one theme. This can provide a focus for your prayer and meditation, too. If you throw in a few Bible verse games that have kids moving as they learn, they may enjoy the time even more. (See the praisefactory.org website for dozens of games like this for preschoolers and for elementary-school age kids.)

3. Full curriculum-based classes

There are a number of great curriculum on the market that help kids understand Bible truths and a structure of redemptive history on a framework of theology. It might be adding in elements to that class time that will prepare them for what they will encounter when they're in the service, such as prayers and learning hymns that they might sing in church or other songs they might sing in church. This might include memorizing and learning the meaning of Bible verses. Praise Factory is certainly one of these curriculums.

> **4. Take a Second Look**
>
> Some churches have a morning and an evening service. Sometimes a Wednesday service, too. You can also use one of these additional services to review what they learned in church, similarly to what was described in number 1 listed above, only as a response to what they learned.

Sunday School Hour: Preparing and Equipping Parents

The Sunday School hour is a great time to equip parents and teachers (and everyone else, too). These classes most certainly may include classes that directly equip them for parenting in the pew or at home. But really, any classes that help parents to know God and His truth better can help them train their children better, whether it be an inductive Bible study or a class in theology, world religions or evangelism. Life with children will take parents to every arena of thought. CHBC offers its Core Seminar "Sunday School" courses for free online. These can be used to train parents or even for parents to use with their children, in a simpler fashion, at home.

Last, but not least, membership classes are a great refresher for parents as their children show signs of conversion and possible interest in baptism. These classes can help parents teach children what it means to be a follower of Christ and a member of a local church.

Classes During the Worship Service: Still Preparing for the Gathering

Other times, churches provide teaching during all or part of the worship service, too.

We mentioned under "Providing For the Gathering" good reasons why you might also offer classes during part or even all of the worship service for younger children. When not treated as a stove-pipe, but as a ramp to gathering together based on developmental ability, these, too, can prepare children for gathering together. This is especially true when you include worship service-like elements in the curriculum.

Praise Factory curriculum does this. Learn more about this family of three, free curriculums at praisefactory.org. But it is not hard to add these elements into most any good curriculum, if they are not already included in it as written. You can even look around the Praise Factory website and curriculum to get some ideas of what you could do to enhance the curriculum you use to better prepare children to gather with the rest of the church.

Doctrine that Matches the Gathering

Whatever the extra teaching you choose, and whomever you intend to teach, it is important that the pastors are part of planning what happens in these classes. They are the overseers of the church. God has entrusted them with teaching sound doctrine. They need to make sure that the teaching helps prepare children for what they're going to experience in the service; and, that the content of the materials used in those classes matches the soundness of doctrine they preach from the pulpit. It means carefully choosing and training teachers who know and can convey these truths to the children. And, it means making sure that curriculum and teachers understand the special developmental challenges in sharing the gospel with children. Sharing the gospel with kids is not exactly the same as sharing with adults. Children feel the weight of pleasing adults and peers that can lead to them wanting to profess faith in Christ even if they truly are not converted. They may not fully understand or feel the weight of conversion and discipleship until they are teenagers. This is not to say that many children are not indeed converted at a tender age. It just means that we need to proceed with care and understanding; with encouragement and patient waiting, before we recognize them as ready for the baptismal pool and the handshake of membership. Let the tender shoots mature and bear timely fruit. Teachers may not know this about children. Make sure to teach them this for the sake of the children and the church.

Church-Shaped Children's Ministry Protects Volunteers for the Worship Gathering at Church

Children's ministry is notorious for either being a hiding place for those who don't want to go to the church service or for being a burn-out place for those who want to make sure there are always enough volunteers to staff the children's ministry programs. Both of these types of people need to be protected from themselves by the pastors.

Pastors Lead the Way

- They make sure that the number of programs you provide matches the sustainable number of volunteers available, so that no one is being asked to serve to frequently for their own spiritual good.

- They set healthy limits on how frequently someone volunteers.

- They set up teaching priorities for whatever these programs are so that if there becomes a regular pattern of insufficient volunteers, they know to limit or even cut out a program of a lower teaching priority, to be able to continue sustaining the programs of higher teaching priority.

Different Churches, Different Priorities

Different churches will have a different set of teaching priorities. For us, our elders have decided that the number one group who needs the most support is parents with infants and toddlers during the worship services. That's taking care of those with children least able to understand what's going on in the service and whose parents are those usually least able to hear because of the noisy, little darlings. Programs for older children are a lower teaching priority because these children are more able to understand, and their parents will be more likely to hear even with their children present.

When space allows, a church also may decide to provide a special room for parents with small, noisy people in tow to watch the service in a space where their children can be noisy without distracting everyone else. For them, they may rather spend their volunteers on teaching children's classes… The kind of classes that help prepare the children for the gathering.

That's why church-shaped children's ministry will always be particular to your particular church. Your elders will assess how to best support your families.

There have been times at CHBC when, even though we had a high percentage of members volunteering, we still have had to completely cut out a program. (This was especially true right after we sent out a large church plant.) We just didn't have a regularly sustainable number of volunteers for the same number of programs. So, the elders looked at the teaching priorities and got rid of Sunday school until we could make up we could get back up to a regular sustainable number of volunteers for that program. They did this to protect having enough volunteers for child care during the worship services. As numbers improved, Sunday School came back class by class, not the whole thing at once. After a year, we were able to bring back all of the classes.

Church-Shaped Children's Ministry Patiently Waits to Fully Participate in the Worship Gathering at Church

We hope that all children will in some way participate along with their parents in the worship service. We hope they will hear the gospel, understand what it means to be a disciple, and as they grow in maturity, become known, not just to their parents but to the church in general, as followers of Christ. We firmly believe that even very young children can understand the gospel and put their trust in Jesus.

How Children Are Different

But, we also firmly believe that children typically mature in a slow cooker kind of way. They are not adults in small clothes. They are adults in the making. And that "making" has well-recognized phases to it.

> **The Classic Trivium of Child Development**
>
> 1. First, a great memory and ability to recall things before they can understand. Hearts that are eager to please and desirous to understand. **(2-10 years old)**
>
> 2. Next, it gives their minds that interact with their memories and their hearts and begin to make connections, taking truth and making it theirs. **(11-13 year olds)**
>
> 3. Then, their wills to full fruition able to make costly decisions for their lives and bear the way of it. **(14-18 year olds)**

As you can see, most children do not get to that third stage of the will until they are well into their teenage years. Some need even more time than that. A few, less. That's why in church-shaped children's ministry, the pastors encourage patient waiting with children who seem to have put their faith in Christ. These pastors choose not to baptize children upon their first vocalization of faith in Christ, but to continue to encourage them in the gospel, in discipleship, and to grow in maturity until they have reached the clear stage of the will. They want to see these children feel the tug of the world, choose Christ, and decide to live in a way that is obviously Christ-centered. And importantly, they want this choice to be obvious not just to their parents, but the church. In this way, baptism is not tied so much to a possible conversion date with young children, but to clear signs of disciple behavior. "Make disciples" Jesus commanded in Matthew 28. This approach wants to see that they are indeed "made" before baptizing, and welcoming these souls to take the Lords Supper, become church members, and most sobering of all, be subject, if necessary to not just parental disciple, but church discipline., if necessary.

It may seem hard to ask children to wait, but their willingness to wait and patiently persevere in the faith for maybe even years to be baptized. But, it is a first good step in showing their willingness to trust the wisdom of their elders, even when they don't completely understand or are happy about it. This will be the first of many times when they will have to do this when they become church members. Willingness to wait patiently and persevere in growing is a great indication of conversion. And, it's a wonderful way of helping the church's witness stay purer; and, for a child's assurance of faith to show itself to be based in reality.

CHURCH-SHAPED CHILDREN'S MINISTRY PATIENTLY WAITS TO FULLY PARTICIPATE IN THE GATHERING

This understanding of children's developmental phases is important for parents and teachers to understand. Learning how to hold out the gospel and invite them to repent and believe, accepting their prayers of faith, but taking a position of encouragement and waiting does not come easily to these dear caregivers who long

to be assured the children are indeed saved. Pastors serve their families well by teaching on this. Our elders even include teaching upon this in the membership classes. Some parents are so adamant about their children being baptized as soon as they show the first flickers of faith. Being upfront on their position of "patient waiting" helps parents to choose another church if they cannot agree with our approach. (This statement is included at the back of this book.)

Helpful Resources

Elders Positon on the Baptism of Children (included in Appendix A)
Understanding Baptism by Bobbie Jamieson

Appendix E: Church-Shaped Children's Ministry: A Whole Church Affair

Church-Shaped Children's Ministry: Encouraging One Another

We've thought about how Church-shaped children's ministry always strives to keep the worship gathering of the church the main thing; how that gathering is preparation for the Great Gathering of all of God's people; and, how parents are equipped through it to have what they need to go home and continue to train their children in the nurture and admonition of the Lord.

But, as we've noted previously this is not simply an exchange of information or experience between pastors, parents, and kids, with no one else involved, as those who agree with the family-integrated church philosophy might argue. (See the article on this philosophy in Appendix B.) God chose to call His people, the body of Christ. That is not just because Christ bought us and is our Head. Scripture is clear: it is also because we are members who work together to carry out all of God's good plans. We can expect to have different gifts and different needs. We can expect to use those gifts to help care for each others' needs. In Romans, Paul says: "For as in one body we have many members, and the members do not all have the same function, so we, though many, are one body in Christ, and individually members one of another. Having gifts that differ according to the grace given to us, let us use them: if prophecy, in proportion to our faith; if service, in our serving; the one who teaches, in his teaching; the one who exhorts, in his exhortation; the one who contributes, in generosity; the one who leads, with zeal; the one who does acts of mercy, with cheerfulness. --Romans 12:4-8

And in his letter to the Ephesians says this: "Speaking the truth in love, we are to grow up in every way into him who is the head, into Christ, from whom the whole body, joined and held together by every joint with which it is equipped, when each part is working properly, makes the body grow so that it builds itself up in love." --Ephesians 4:15-16

This is God's beautiful plan: to use us to be a picture of Him as we love one another.

Nowhere in Scripture is training up children excluded from the "needy list." And actually, we see verses to the contrary. The very fact that Paul writes to churches for parents to raise their children in God's ways (Ephesians 6) shows a desire for the whole church needs to hear this because they will undoubtedly be helping each other in this task, as passages like Titus 2 points to.

We are not to be family-integrated, unless you are talking about the family which is the body of Christ. We are to be family-equipping, when we speak of our biological families and the church. We help one another to all reach maturity in Christ: "Him we proclaim, warning everyone and teaching everyone with all wisdom, that we may present everyone mature in Christ." --Colossians 1:28

This is church-shaped children's ministry.

But what do the different "members" of the local church work together to equip parents and train up children? There are five, different groups of people, and two, most common places where this equipping take place in the church. The next page shows an overview of these.

> **Church-shaped Children's Ministry**
>
> **Pastors lead their church**
>
> **in serving WHO they have**
> - parents
> - children
>
> **with WHAT they have:**
> - church services
> - programs
> - member volunteers
> - children's ministry leaders
>
> *(living within the spiritually- healthy limits, these imply)*
>
> **that ALL might gather,**
>
> **for the good of the WHOLE church,**
>
> **and to the GLORY of God.**

Now we are going to look at church-shaped ministry, segment by segment: the part each plays in church-shaped children's ministry, special care to bear in mind with each, and ideas on how to better encourage one another.

Pastors Take the Lead in Shaping Children's Ministry for the Good of the Whole Congregation

Church-shaped Children's Ministry starts with the pastors.

How pastors lead their church in ministering to children has a far more significant impact on both their present and future members than they might first imagine. Pastors are accountable before God for sound teaching in their local church, even for sound teaching in children's ministry.

Pastors love, lead, limit; preach, pray, protect; equip and encourage the congregation as they work together to raise the children in their midst in the nurture and admonition of the Lord. **Pastors, your ministry IS children's ministry!**

WHAT PASTORS CAN DO

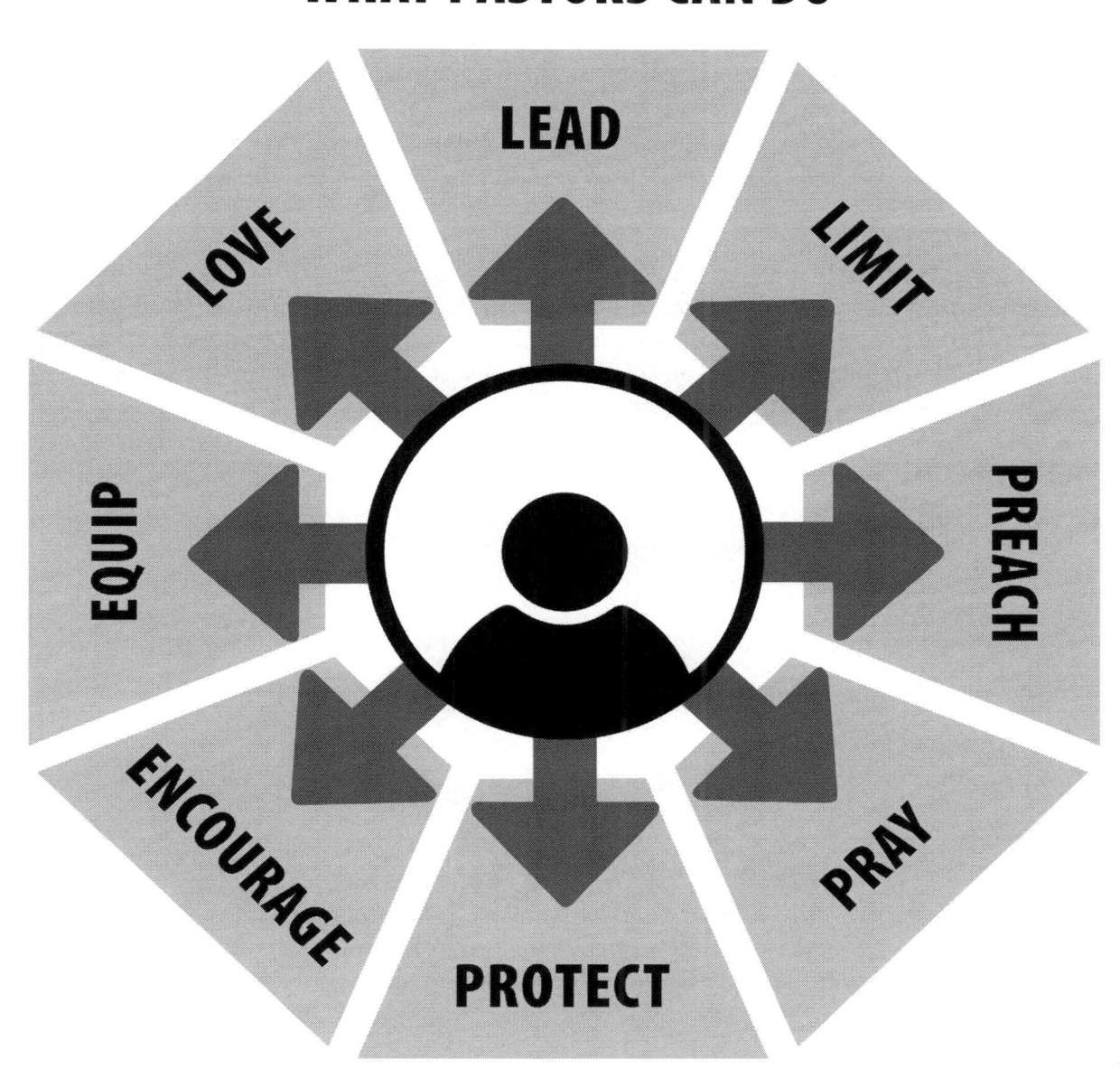

- LEAD
- LOVE
- LIMIT
- EQUIP
- PREACH
- ENCOURAGE
- PRAY
- PROTECT

What Pastors Can Do

LEAD →

BY EXAMPLE
- They lead by example in how they raise their children. Not as models of perfection, but as faithful and godly fathers, depending upon the Lord to help them parent their children well. This is a qualification for being a pastor, elder or deacon.

BY VISION-CASTING
- They provide the vision for what to teach adults and children in any teaching outside of the pulpit. They set these in order of priority and make them available as the number of volunteers becomes sustainable.

- They handle the most difficult conversations with parents or teachers that arise in the children's programs.

BY HUMBLE, WISDOM-BASED DECISION MAKING
- They take advice and ask questions. Pastoral leadership does not mean that no guidance will be needed to make good decisions. The best leaders are humble learners. Pastors will need the wise insights of the children's ministry team, parents, teachers, and others to make the best decisions for the whole church. With many advisers, come the best decisions!

BY LOOKING AT THE BIG PICTURE
- They consider how to help everyone to gather together for worship. They want to support parents so they can grow and be equipped to train their children. They think about how to use the church service and carefully choose classes to provide a ramp up for the children to that gathering. But they do so, always keeping a watchful eye out for those who serve us in children's ministry, that they might not overserve.

BY REGULAR CHECK-UPS
- They are known as the church's leaders of children's ministry and take responsibility for it in knowing what is going on and giving regular guidance.

BY BEING INVOLVED
- They handle the most difficult conversations with parents or teachers that arise in the children's programs.

BY PASTORING FAMILIES
- They provide pastoral oversight of families, programs, and children's ministry volunteers.

BY A LIAISON
- They choose one elder/pastor as liaison, overseer, and encourager of children's ministry and its leadership. He receives regular updates on families, volunteers, programs, curriculum changes, and arising issues. He takes charge of difficult situations and bears the burden of enforcing unpopular but needful actions. He reports back to the other pastors, so they can pray, advise, and care well for those involved, too.

LOVE →

- They love and care for the flock under their care, from the youngest to the oldest.

- They discuss, guide, and pray with parents having difficulties with their children.

- They think about how to care well for the children who come to church without their parents.

- They take time to speak to children from the pulpit and in person.

- They can show love to their own children.

LIMIT →

- Establish volunteer serving limits to ensure that all volunteers are also being well-fed themselves.

- Decide on a healthy, sustainable number of classes/programs to offer, balancing needs with available budget and volunteers.

PREACH →

- Feed parents and children from the regular preaching of God's Word.

- Urge the congregation to serve each other in children's ministry in your applications when is appropriate.

- Are a part of making decisions about curriculum soundness and teacher qualifications for any classes offered to adults or children that they do not personally teach. The curriculum and the teachers are an extension of their authority to preach into the hands (and mouths) of others. They want to be careful that this preaching is sound.

PRAY →

- Take time to regularly pray through the membership, including families.

- Pray with parents facing challenges.

- Realize that many of the church's future members and leaders are in their midst now as children. Pray for the future church today.

PROTECT →

- Make sure that an effective child protection policy to keep children and volunteers safe BEFORE any childcare takes place. Abuse scars children and destroys a church's ministry.

- Set wise guidelines for the baptism of children and their partaking of the Lord's Supper, protecting children from false assurance of salvation and the church from unconverted members.

ENCOURAGE →

- Encourage parents in their calling to raise their children in the nurture and the admonition of the Lord.

- Encourage the congregation to pursue honest conversation concerning their parenting struggles, building one another up with wise words and helpful service.

- Encourage children who profess Christ at an early age to keep on growing in discipleship and patiently wait for the best time to be baptized and join the church.

EQUIP →

- Appoint a like-minded administrator/team to implement the pastors' vision.

- Lead the church in recognizing deacons of children's ministry who support the administrator and the teachers/nursery workers as they serve.

- Equip parents, children, and their teachers through the regular preaching of God's Word.

- Equip parents through adult classes, raising their biblical knowledge or their parenting knowledge that they can use to train up their children.

- Equip parents and teachers with an understanding of conversion in children. Help them to know how to share the gospel with children and encourage them in discipleship, while being aware that children are best served by waiting until youth/young adulthood for signs of Christian maturity that is recognizable by the whole church and stands the test of temptation and persecution.

- Make book recommendations for parents to read or read to their children.

- If you give away books during the service (like we do weekly), make some of them kids' books and give them to the kids directly. Tell the child who receives it that you would love for them to draw a picture or come tell you what they thought about it later.

Parents Are the Primary, Spiritual Caregivers of Their Children

Church-shaped Children's Ministry recognizes parents as the primary, spiritual caregivers of their children. The Bible is filled with passages encouraging parents to raise up their children in the nurture and admonition in the Lord (Ephesians 6:4; Deuteronomy 4:9, 11:19; Isaiah 38:19; Joel 1:3; Psalm 78:4). Men being considered for roles as elder, deacon and pastor must first be good leaders of their families in the home (1 Timothy 3:4). God clearly takes the call to teach our children His ways very seriously, for the children's sake and for the sake of His Church.

Spiritually caring for children is no easy task. God equips parents for it through His Word, read at home and taught at church. They parent by the power of the Holy Spirit, and with the help and encouragement of the pastors and fellow members of their local church. They train up their children through the gatherings of the church as well as at home.

But just because parents are the primary spiritual caregivers, does not mean they have to spiritually care for their children alone. As members of a local church of covenanting believers, Church-shaped Children's Ministry seeks to encourage parents in this daunting task in ways that support, without usurping their special calling. Every family is different. This support is respectful of differences in approach parents may have for taking care of their children's spiritual needs. It is also sensitive to the different needs of different families. Some parents are younger Christians or single parents. These may need the most support of all. (See Appendix B for my response to the family-integrated church ideology which begs to differ.)

Supporting parents can take on various forms: from honest sharing, advice-giving, and prayer among members; to recommending resources for parents to use as they train their children in gospel truths at home; to providing safe childcare while parents attend classes or workshops; to preaching to them from the pulpit; as well as to offering Bible classes and youth group for the children, themselves.

Why Parents Make Your Ministry Children's Ministry

Your Ministry IS Children's Ministry, as the local church raises up and equips those who will be primary, spiritual caregivers of children.

Most of those who attend your church are or will be parents, at one point in their lives. Parenting will be one of their greatest, God-given callings... and challenges.

Parents help their children take part in church services. They help them understand the prayers, music, ordinances, and the reading and preaching of God's Word. Frequently, a parent's attention is divided between training their child and focusing on the worship service. This requires much patience.

Parents vary in their own Bible and parenting knowledge. Some are better equipped than others to spiritually nurture their children. Everyone needs help and encouragement!

What Churches Can Do

1. Fill Your Parents at Church

- Fill your parents with solid preaching that they grow from themselves as well as pass on to their kids.

- Provide parenting workshop/classes or mentoring relationships to encourage parents, especially new parents.

2. Remind Your Parents

- Remind parents from the pulpit of their calling as the primary, spiritual care-givers of their children.

3. Provide Resources

- Recommend resources that can help children engage in the worship services (bulletins, notebooks, etc.).

- Provide Sunday School take-home sheets for parents to reinforce these truths at home. Provide a booklist of great books parents can use to teach their children about God.

- Have a bookstall or a library of resources parents know they can count on.

- Have a bookfair to display good resources parents might not know about.

4. Encourage One Another

- Encourage members to honestly share, pray, and seek advice from the pastors and from each other for their parenting needs and struggles.

- Hold panel discussions on various topics related to parenting and children.

- Encourage members to appreciate different styles in parenting and schooling that may differ in approach but lead to the same biblically-based goals.

5. Provide Help with the Kids

- Provide child care for babies and toddlers during adult teaching times, so parents can listen well themselves.

- Offer Bible classes for children. These can provide helpful support to parents' teaching, as well as allow the children to see the work of God's grace in the lives of their teachers.

6. Help Them Understand How Kids Are Different

- Equip parents with appropriate language and developmental knowledge for conversion and children.

- Help them understand how children are different in needing a longer period of time to mature and show the fruit of true conversion.

- Help them learn how to point their children to Christ and encourage their growth in discipleship, even as they wait for baptism, the Lord's Supper and church membership.

Children: Tomorrow's Church in Your Midst Today

Realizing that childhood is an especially responsive time of learning, and even conversion and spiritual growth, Church-Shaped Children's Ministry seeks to make the most of these years. In conversations, in classes, in resources, in worship services, church members seek to clearly proclaim the gospel to the children, as well as live out the gospel before them.

The members of a local church gather together each week to worship God and love one another. They seek this gathering to be a picture of the beautiful love of Christ for His Church that glorifies God. They hope this picture will remain in children's hearts and minds as a winsome testimony to the gospel. They also help teach these children God's Word, leaving a legacy of truth in their minds. And that, Lord willing, the Holy Spirit can ripen in their hearts, bring them to a saving knowledge of Christ, and prepare them one day to be well-equipped to commit themselves as followers of Christ and lovers of His Church, as well.

Childhood is a rich time to equip children with gospel truths that can prepare them for life, godliness, and for gathering together as church members, themselves, one day.

Why Children Make Your Ministry Children's Ministry

Here are three very good reasons:

- Everyone who attends your church was or is a child. Your current members and leaders WERE children. Your future members and leaders ARE children now.

- The highest concentration of non-Christians attending your church is usually the children in your children's programs.

- The "4-14" age window is the most common age of conversion. It is also when kids are most prone to "make decisions" to please their parents or teachers, without being truly converted.

What Churches Can Do

1. Include Them in the Worship Gatherings

- Include the children in your worship gatherings. They need to hear God's Word through preaching. They need to see the body of Christ worshipping and reflecting its Head. If you do have classes for younger children, make sure to phase these out and gradually include the children in the service. Do not "stove pipe" them from one separate service to another, never bringing them into the service.

- Pastors, be mindful of the children in your services, either indirectly, by providing a simple sermon outline or easy-to-understand illustrations; or, even directly, by addressing them at some point in your sermon with a question or an application.

- Provide blank paper or a simple outline or another form of worship service aid for the children to use. Truth 78 has some particularly useful resources.

- If your pastor give away books during the service, make some of them kids' books and give them to the kids directly. Have the pastor tell the child who receives it that he would love for them to draw a picture or come tell him what they thought about it later.

2. Pray for Them and Their Families
- Pray for families. Include a section in your membership directory listing parents and the names/ages of children. This helps the congregation easily and regularly pray for them.

3. Care for Them While Their Parents Learn in Their Own Classes or in the Worship Service
- There is great value in having the children in the worship service. This is the goal of church-shaped children's ministry. But there is also something to be said for giving parents a chance to learn and worship undistracted. This is especially true when the children are very young and unable to pay attention themselves.

- Providing safe childcare for infants and toddlers can be a great way to strengthen parents as well as equip them with truth to teach their children at home. It may feel like babysitting, but this is really serving the preaching of the Word.

- If your church provides care for preschoolers (and maybe even young, elementary-school age children) during part or all of the worship service, you can double the value by teaching these older children Bible truths during this time.

4. Be a Witness
- Provide children with a faithful testimony of life with God as they see God's work of grace in the lives of their parents, teachers, and other members.

5. Help Disciple Them and Prepare Them for the Worship Gathering
- Share the gospel with children so the lost might be saved. Make disciples of those who trust in Christ.

- Offer Bible classes for children. These can reinforce what Christian parents teach at home, as well as introduce God's truths to children from non-Christian homes. These can leave a legacy of Bible truth in young hearts that echoes throughout their lives.

- Prepare children to gather together with the members of your local church in their classes by helping them make a connection between what they are learning in class and what they will take part in the service.

- Mentor non-Christian kids who attend your church without their parents. Wrap both them and their parents into your families as a display of the goodness and love of God.

6. Be Mindful of Their Developmental Differences
- Treat children as the work in progress that they are. The church knows this and cares for them with patience, love, perseverance, and prayer. The Lord may use what the children learn and watch while they are young, or one day, many years to come.

- Make disciples, not baptismal statistics. "Pleasing" can mimic true conversion in the short run. Look for sustained fruit before you baptize. Out of care for a child's soul and for the church's pure witness, pastors encourage patiently waiting for young faith to bear mature fruit, so as not to confuse childish eagerness with true conversion.

7. Treat Them with Kindness and Gentleness

- Children are impressionable. They remember how they are treated. They notice how others live, and emulate (or try not to) them. Create a winsome memory of Christ and His church by treating children with love, respect, and kindness.

- Don't exasperate children who aren't "Bible memory stars." Make understanding the truth, not getting it word perfect, the point.

8. Get to Know Them and Enjoy Them

- Do not underestimate the value of taking time to talk to children. This is true for every member of the church, but especially pastors. Kids open like flowers when you show you are interested in their lives. They love to know you care. Even the most basic conversations can build a foundation of receptivity that the Lord may use later to commend the gospel to this very same child.

The Church:
Equipping Families
Through the Worship Gathering

"After this I looked, and behold, a great multitude that no one could number, from every nation, from all tribes and peoples and languages, standing before the throne and before the Lamb, clothed in white robes, with palm branches in their hands, and crying out with a loud voice, "Salvation belongs to our God who sits on the throne, and to the Lamb!" Revelation 7:9-10, ESV

This is the great Day that God's people yearn for. This is the great Day for which we share the gospel and urge all to accept. And this is the Day of which we have a little dress rehearsal each Lord's Day we gather together to worship God and love one another. Once a week, we are all together-- our own, little version of every nation, tribe, people, and languages praising God. So very different, in so many ways, yet unified by our Head and beloved Savior, Christ. This a dress rehearsal that we want to our children to watch and take part in. There is a special reflection of Christ that can be seen in these gatherings of God's people. We don't want our children to miss it.

But in this day when custom, same-age learning is so highly esteemed, sometimes the importance of including children in the church's weekly gathering together is downplayed, if not left out almost completely. Unfortunately, the well-intentioned customization can create a diversion from exposure to the whole church body gatherings that starts with children's church, continues with youth church, then ends with college ministry. It may not be until they are adults that they have much opportunity to see the beauty of gathering together with others different from us and learn how to be a part of that, themselves. They miss the chance to gradually become familiar with, and hopefully come to love, these gatherings.

Church-shaped Children's Ministry also sees the great benefit of customized, same-age teaching times. It may include--even often include-- nursery child care as well as classes for younger kids, not only during a separate Sunday School hour, but even during all or part of the worship services. BUT, the eye is always on the goal: everyone gathering together to worship God and hear the preaching of the Word. It sets a path that gradually leads all to this point and offers parents resources to help their kids along the way.

Why the Worship Gathering Is Children's Ministry

The Bible Tells Me So
The worship gathering is the "main thing" of any local church. Parents being equipped and children being trained up through the worship gathering is the basic, biblical model of children's ministry. Anything else that a church provides as children's ministry should flow to and from the worship gathering.

Everybody's Doing It
Most congregations include a high percentage of families who are parenting their kids in the pew.

Why It's Hard to Decide What to Do
Different elements of the worship service are more quickly understood and accessible to younger children. Children vary a lot in their ability to sit still, listen and understand. Different approaches will be needed to help these different children gather well with the congregation.

A Lot of Opinions

Families can have very different, strongly held opinions on how and when to include their children in the worship services. These strong opinions can sometimes cause friction with others who do not hold to their opinion. This can cause divisiveness.

Missing in Action

Volunteers who serve in child-care and Bible classes that take part during the worship services miss the opportunity to gather together with the congregation.

Substitute Services

Many times, children's church and youth church strives to provide a very different, "more exciting" experience than the whole congregation worship service. They do not prepare the children well to take part in the church life that will be offered to them in their adult life.

Furthermore, many times children/youth "church" enlists kids who are not necessarily believers as part the "worship team" or to take other up-front roles that are meant only for mature, Christian leaders. This is not a healthy or a good model of what it means to gather as a church.

What Churches Can Do

1. Be Family-Friendly

- Provide a "cry" room with audio/video feed for parents with children who are noisy while "in-training." This allows for the training to continue without the worry of distracting others.

- Provide audio feed of the service into the nursing mothers' room, if you have one. Or, provide an area in the back of the hall for nursing moms to nurse in a less prominent location, but still able to be a part of the service. (Some church plants in temporary sites, such as hotel ballrooms or school auditioriums, have even put up a portable partition in the back of the area with seats for nursing moms behind it.)

- Provide worship service aids for use during the services. Children Desiring God has some great, little, spiral-bound books that can be used with any worship service. They can be used at home to hold a "service" review discussion on truths learned.

- Pastors address the children in the application portions of their sermons, reminding children that this message is for them, too.

2. Trading Ideas

- Provide resources and even hold a panel on parenting in the pew. Make sure to include not just "successful parents" of "well-behaved" children, if you do the panel. Those even-tempered children are the not nearly as common as we might like to think. It will be the parents with the wiggly, inattentive, strong-willed kids who are attempting this that will be most encouraging to those who attend. Victorious overcomer parents are a thing of beauty, but the ones who remain in the war zone despite all odds are the ones who may have the best advice and provide the most encouragement for struggling parents.

3. Respect for Differences

- Create an atmosphere that allows for "different strokes for different folks". Help your parents appreciate each other and encourage each other, even when they are choosing a different approach for preparing their children to gather together.

4. Start at Home

- At home, family worship time can include songs sung at church. They also can take home a service bulletin and use it in their worship time.

5. Cooperative Classroom

- Choose curriculum or adapt your curriculum to include "ramp-up" to worship service elements in the children's classes. This can be easily done by including hymns or other worship songs into the schedule and taking time to explain the meaning of the words.

- Introduce the children to the leaders whom they will see up front leading the congregation by inviting them to come to the class and talk with the kids. Familiarity with the leaders can really help kids be more interested in what is going on. We (Capitol Hill Baptist Church) have added a "VIPP" (Very Important Prayer Person) activity into our classes for elementary-school aged children. They learn about what different leaders in the church do (learn words like deacon, elder, pastor, etc.), what they do and how to pray for them. But they also learn fun things like what each person likes to do in their free time and what is their favorite food and animal. This helps the children connect with these leaders as people, not just as figure heads.

6. Loving Limits

- Pastors set healthy volunteering limits to make sure all child-care volunteers get to gather together with the congregation on a regular basis.

- Pastors with the helpful input of children's ministry leaders and others, look at how they can set age limits on any child-care/Bible classes that take place during any worship service. They will want to weigh length of service (especially preaching time) as well as understandability of the service elements as they consider what (if any) childcare/classes to offer children during all/part of the service. The idea is to create an up-ramp that eventually includes the children for the entire congregational gathering. They will also want to think about what parents might most benefit from child care offered during the worship service. Frequently, this may look like care for babies (childcare, no teaching) during the whole service, as well as classes for preschoolers and/or younger elementary school children during the sermon portion of the service. Teachers and parents also look for signs of readiness for children to stay in the whole service. Parents may choose to have their children stay in for the sermon some weeks but go out for their sermon-time class others.

7. Take Care with Special Services

- If you do have a special worship time for children/youth, make sure it echoes the gathering together of the church. Include prayers and songs that they will also sing with the whole congregation. Make sure godly, mature leaders, not the children, lead the worship times. If at all possible, gradually phase these special services out if they are seen as substitutes to the gathering of the whole church.

- Help support and/or welcome Campus Outreach within your church. It is a college outreach organization that is church based. Not only do they work on campus with college students, but they encourage them to become an active member of a local church. This sets these students up well to be members of a local church after they graduate.

Programs: Supporting the Preaching in Sustainable Ways

Programs partner with the preaching so that all members might be fed, parents equipped, and children might be better trained up for life, godliness, and gathering with God's people. They do not replace the worship service, but aid it, in a variety of ways.

Some Benefits of Programs in Children's Ministry

Help Feed Parents So They Can Feed Their Children

These support programs can make a huge difference to parents, allowing them to hear God's Word and understand how to live it out, for the good of their own souls and the good of their children. Even the most basic, safe childcare can multiply the power of God's Word in the lives of families, simply by making it possible for parents to learn undistractedly themselves.

Teaching at Church Transfers to Home

These programs can also be a great aid in teaching parents (and future parents) how to talk to their children about God. For children from non-Christian or new Christian homes, these programs may provide the teaching they do not get at home. Children of believers can also learn truths that support what their parents teach at home.

Winsome Witness

They provide a regular opportunity for members to be a witness for the gospel in their time teaching children in the classroom. Their love for God, His Word, His people, and for them (the kids), can be a powerful display of God's love, power, and goodness to the children.

Ramp-up to the Worship Gathering

They can provide a ramp-up to the worship service by teaching children truths that help them better understand what they see and hear in the service.

Some "Bewares" of Programs in Children's Ministry

Cost of Up-keep

Children's Ministry programs frequently enlist more volunteers than any other ministry in the church. Once a Children's Ministry program is offered, the expectation is high to keep it going, sometimes, even at the expense of what is spiritually best for your volunteer teachers. It is important to make sure these volunteers are well-cared for spiritually, themselves. And, it's important to count the cost of recruiting and maintaining a sustainable volunteer schedule before you add any new program. Go slowly!

Shiny Package, Good Theology?

Sadly, the most kid-friendly, exciting, published curriculums are not always the most biblically sound. The "wow" factor of these curriculums can be very attractive, but can lead to unbiblical, simply moralistic, teaching. Read the curriculum carefully before purchasing!

Family Time Crunch

Sometimes, children's ministry programs become so numerous as to crowd out important family time.

What Churches Can Do

Pastors Lead the Way

- Pastors choose programs as part of the teaching of God's Word in the church under their care. They set teaching priorities and approve curriculum choices for Children's Ministry programs.

- They decide which programs the church will implement, taking into consideration need, family time, available budget, and the number of volunteers needed. Care for the WHOLE church--families and volunteers-- is of prime concern to the pastors, and directly affects what programs are offered and when.

- Healthy spiritual growth for and healthy sustainability for the whole church, not a program's attractiveness or its potential to swell attendance, drives their decisions.

- Children's ministry leaders, teachers, parents, and others can help the pastors understand their biggest needs in being better equipped to spiritually care for the children. Pastors can regularly seek the wisdom of these people to make the best decisions for the whole church.

Keep the Gathering the Main Thing

- Always keep the worship gathering in view. Choose programs that will prepare the children for these gatherings. Time the programs so that they do not conflict with the gatherings unless they directly support it (such as childcare for infants and toddlers.) Programs like these will always be phased out so that children are gathering with God's people as much as possible, as soon as possible. The gathering is always the goal.

Support, Don't Usurp

- Programs support, not replace, the parents' own spiritual training of their children.

Small Is Beautiful

- Start small. Offer less. Only add more, slowly.

- In some very small churches, the programs supporting parents might look as bare bones as regularly praying for parents; encouraging them and their children from the pulpit during the worship service; recommending good resources to use with their children in the pew and at home; and, facilitating honest conversations among fellow members.

- When you feel you cannot offer a particular program at church, recommend resources that parents can use to teach these same truths to their children at home.

Re-visit, Re-evaluate

- Pastors determine when to add, close, or modify programs. They teach members to expect some ebb and flow in programs to care well for the spiritual needs of all --volunteers and families alike.

PROGRAMS: SUPPORTING THE PREACHING IN SUSTAINABLE WAYS

- Sometimes the volunteer pool or the budget shrinks. Or, there are so many kids, that the church can no longer provide the same number of programs or for the same group of children. The church shape has changed again, and the leaders respond to these changes, trying to continue to care well for everyone. This might mean only offering classes for K-6th grade, when previously you offered classes for K-12th grade. It might mean putting a cap on the number of children you have in a classroom, rather than over-taxing volunteers beyond what is good for them.

- As the church expands, the pastors re-visit what might be beneficial to the growing congregation and what is now possible with the increased resources on hand. It very well could expand to a bookstall of resources for family devotions, childcare for babies, and Sunday School classes for parents and children on all or most Sundays. From there, it might grow to include many other programs. But always, whatever is done, the pastors take into consideration healthy limits for the spiritual well-being of all.

Member Volunteers: Supporting Parents in Sustainable Ways

Member volunteers support and encourage parents by helping to care, teach, and mentor their children through the local church. They provide the children with a testimony of God's grace through their lives. They serve within limits set by elders, to meet the needs of children's ministry, but not at the expense of their own spiritual nurturing. They may serve in "over-sized" teams that don't require every teacher to teach every session to share the teaching load, avoid burnout, and provide natural substitute teachers for classes. They are a great way to train less-inexperienced teachers by pairing them with more experienced lead teachers.

Church-shaped Children's Ministry strives to care for the spiritual well-being of all church members, not just the families. What programs you offer should be directly influenced by who you are and what resources you have. You need to live within this "budget" for the spiritual health of all your members. Building size, number of willing and qualified teachers, age and number of children; available finances; maturity of the Christian parents (ability to teach their children truths, themselves), number of services, and many other factors should be taken into consideration.

Membership Matters in Children's Ministry

Ministry to Parents as Well as Kids

Fellow members join together with parents in providing the children with a testimony of God's grace through their lives. Members support and encourage parents by mentoring each other, and by helping to care, teach, and mentor their children through the local church.

Major Teaching Responsibility

There are often more teachers, teaching more souls, in children's ministry than in any venue in your church, outside of the pulpit. Most Sunday School teachers are not trained teachers or preachers. Curriculum doesn't just teach children. It often is teaching your teachers, too.

Typical Troubles

Over-volunteering and under-training are usually the two, biggest reasons why volunteers do not come back. Typically, more members miss the worship services and adult classes because of children's ministry obligations than any other ministry of the church. Children's ministry programs can be vulnerable places for child abuse to occur in the local church, especially when there is no child protection policy in place.

MEMBER VOLUNTEERS: SUPPORTING PARENTS IN SUSTAINABLE WAYS

What Churches Can Do

1. Include with Care

- Carefully screen and train members for working with the children. Make sure volunteers comply with the church's child protection policy for their own good, the good of the children, and the good of the church.

2. Love within Limits

- Have members serve in children's classes within limits set by elders, to meet the needs of children's ministry, but not at the expense of members' own spiritual nurturing.

3. Help Your Teachers

- Provide pastor-approved curriculum that is biblically solid, developmentally-appropriate, and teacher-friendly.

- Know your teachers before they teach. Pair more-experienced, better-known teachers, with newer, lesser-known teachers. Require a waiting period before brand-new members can work directly with kids..

- Provide teachers with mentors who can teach them how to manage a classroom, as well as engage children in ways that are understandable, memorable, and enjoyable.

- Enlist "oversized" teaching teams for each program (not everyone teaches every week). This helps avoid teacher burnout; builds in vacation time and good, substitute teacher choices, and it allows for teachers to regularly attend adult classes and worship services.

Children's Ministry Leaders: Carrying Out the Pastors' Vision

Children's Ministry Administrators (and other CM leaders) work under the leadership of the pastors. They bring the pastoral vision to life through the curriculum they implement, the volunteers they help train and enlist, and by generally encouraging families. They provide regular updates to keep the pastors informed, so they can care well for families and volunteers.

The Load-Bearers in Children's Ministry

- These carry most of the huge burden of enlisting, training, and managing teachers; finding (or creating) good curriculum; and, caring well for the needs of many, different families.

- Sometimes they are poorly led by the pastors who do not carefully consider what the church is able to do. They pass down new programs to these leaders like "un-funded mandates" who are supposed to carry out their vision without volunteers available to fulfill them.

- They are often the "on-call, bad cop" who enforces difficult but necessary policies for everyone's good. They are often the "stopgap" for last-minute substitutes and other classroom issues. If there's a need, they are called to meet it. They can become so busy filling urgent needs, that their own spiritual needs are neglected.

A Children's Ministry Administrator who lasts more than a few years is a very rare bird, indeed.

What Churches Can Do

1. The Buck Doesn't Stop Here: Regular, Pastoral Oversight

- Have a designated pastor who oversees and encourages the whole children's ministry team. He schedules regular meetings with the team to keep informed and to know how he and the other pastors can best care for the leaders, teachers, and families involved. He initiates any needed pastoral conversations with children ministry workers, teachers, or parents. He shares the job of enforcing difficult policies. He reviews and approves any curriculum choices. He reports back to the other pastors for their prayers, input, and further oversight.

2. A Little R & R

- Shepherd your CMA and deacons well by ensuring they regularly attend worship services. CMA's need regular vacation breaks, too. Well-trained assistants and program team leaders can help your programs run smoothly, even in their absence.

3. Helping Hands

- Recognize children's ministry deacons who work alongside the Children's Ministry Administrator/team (CMA) to welcome families, support teachers, and otherwise keep children's ministry programs running smoothly on Sundays or other program days. They are a great help to families, teachers, and the CMA.

- Designate children's ministry team leaders to take over much of the CMA's burden of finding substitutes and other last-minute program issues.

Your Ministry IS Children's Ministry!

Do you see how Children's Ministry takes on a significant role in your church? Its impact on the congregation can be felt far outside of the Sunday School classroom walls. That's why we say that your ministry IS children's ministry. Because in one way, shape or form, everyone in your church is affected.

And that's why, children's ministry, which can seem like such a sideline ministry, needs pastoral leadership. And if you give it the leadership it needs, it can bear much good fruit in your church now and in the future.

So far, we've talked a lot of theology, church history, and theory. Now it's time to look at some practical examples. First, I'll describe what Church-shaped children's ministry looks like at our church, Capitol Hill Baptist Church, under the leadership of our elders. Then, we will look at examples from other churches.

Every church is shaped differently, so that means what you might do at your church will probably look different than what we have done here. But we hope that there will be enough elements that will be helpful to you as you seek out your own shape.

Appendix F:

Capitol Hill Baptist Church

One Example of Church-Shaped Children's Ministry

A Little about Washington, DC and Capitol Hill Baptist Church

Life in Washington, D.C.

Capitol Hill Baptist Church is located in Washington, DC, just a few blocks behind the Capitol. It is a vibrant city, that takes much of its life from the people who come here to take part in our nation's government, as well as many stationed here in military positions. It has an unusually high number of young adults in their 20's. DC is a very transient city, with both politicians and their staff coming and going, as well as military postings that usually last no more than three years. It is also a city of many internationals, coming either for college or for work.

Housing prices are very high. Public schools are not the best (though they are getting better), and the price of private school would astound you. While our church as an unusual number of families who somehow find a way to live close to the church in the Capitol Hill neighborhood, many families wind up moving out to the suburbs for the better, public school and somewhat cheaper housing prices by the time their children reach school age.

Capitol Hill Baptist Church: Where We Live Affects Who We Are

Capitol Hill Baptist Church had its humble beginnings in a prayer meeting on the Hill in 1867. In 1876, it started the Capitol Hill Baptist Sunday School Society. (Yet another reason why our church, in particular, is indebted to children's ministry!) It constituted as a church and began to hold worship services in 1878, a small congregation of 31 members.

How very distant those beginnings seem from our present gathering of members! The personality of the city is reflected in our church. We have a high percentage of young, unmarried/newly married members. Chances are they will move out of the area within three years. We turn over a third of our 900+ membership every few years. Those that do stay, are enthusiastic about their families. Many of them have three or more children. We average about 100 babies born each year. These babies have about 100 preschool siblings, 100 elementary school siblings, and about 50 siblings in middle school and high school. Campus Outreach is based out of our church. Largely through them, around 100 college students attend/become members during their time in college.

We may be heavy in young singles, married, with or without children, but we are "light" in older adults of the empty-nest and older variety. This number is growing as our congregation ages, but we still only have about members, ages forty and older.

Our Leadership
We are an elder-led (not elder-ruled) congregational church. We have 30 elders, as well as 30 deacons who care for the congregation. We have one senior pastor, five associate pastors, two assistant pastors, plus a number of pastoral assistants. We have a full-time, paid Children's Ministry Administrator, a part-time Curriculum Developer/Teacher Trainer, as well as four deacons who support these paid workers and help the member volunteer teachers on Sundays. I (Constance Dever) spend much of my days developing curriculum but am unpaid.

A LITTLE ABOUT WASHINGTON, DC AND CAPITOL HILL BAPTIST CHURCH

Our Membership

You must be a member to join in most of the activities of the church. This is not trying to be exclusive, but it is because we are serious about the covenant we make together. We commit our lives to each other. We live under the loving care of our pastors. We try to actively live out the promises to disciple each other and to encourage each other in whatever callings God has given us, including the raising of our children.

Our Services and Other Programs

We gather together as one body, each Sunday morning for about an hour of music, prayers, and Bible reading, followed by an hour-long, expositional sermon. We meet together again on Sunday evenings for more worship, an extended time of prayer and sharing, and a shorter message (15 minutes) from the opposite testament of the Bible from the morning service, but on a related passage/theme. These evening services are attended by a majority of our membership and provide a wonderful way to bind our lives together and encourage us in the faith in a more intimate fashion than the morning services.

We also have Core Seminar (Sunday School classes) for adults before the Sunday morning worship service, as well as a Wednesday night inductive Bible study. Many members are also involved in small groups (only men or women) or community groups (men and women). The elders have chosen for the church schedule to remain light from other programs. They want the members to have time to care for their families and build relationships with others, especially non-Christians. Members are deliberate about meeting up to enjoy, disciple, and encourage one another.

Overview of Children's Ministry at Capitol Hill Baptist Church

Elders Set Goals

Our Children's Ministry reflect the elders' goals to provide:

- The MOST child-care help is for those parents who will be LEAST to hear because of their children's ages/abilities.

- Teaching that will support, but not usurp the parents' biblical training of their children.

- What will be taught in those classes (Bible, Theology, Discipleship, etc.) and what curriculum will be used to teach it.

- Separate teaching for younger children who might be less likely to understand the sermon.

- Programs that by their content, and by the age limitations to whom they are offered, will create an up-ramp to gathering together with the whole congregation.

Reflects the Needs and Opportunities of Our Own Community
They also reflect the realities of our community. For instance, we hold a one-day, Saturday VBS instead of the traditional full-week version because that's what works best for outreach here on Capitol Hill. And, we do not offer childcare of any kind during our Wednesday evening service because most families typically stay at home on Wednesday nights, either because of school schedules or because they live so far away.

Respect for Differences
Many of our families homeschool, though an increasing number have their children in public (usually Charter) schools or Christian (especially hybrid) schools. At church, we have many parents who include their children in classes/child-care and many who do not. We encourage parents to not set up strongholds of opinions about either of these issues, acting like their school or worship participation choice is the only right way. We agree on the essentials of the gospel. We allow for Christian freedom everywhere else.

Quick to Share Gospel, Slow to Baptize Children
We are quick to share the gospel (in every sermon and every Bible class), but slow to baptize children. The elders have found that it is best for children to be encouraged to grow and become known more broadly within the church as a Christian because pleasing adults can easily mimic conversion in children. This is NOT because the elders think that children cannot become Christians. Many became Christians as children, themselves. It is out of care for the children's souls and for the purity of the church that they have made this decision.

Anyone who is baptized becomes a full member of the church. They go through membership classes like everyone else. Because this can be a hot topic with parents, the elders give out their thought paper on this decision for them to read and understand before they join the church. Better to be up-front about this, than to get what may feel like an unwelcome surprise later. (See the elders' paper on baptism in Appendix A.)

Safe Child Care

We make safe childcare a top priority. Only members can be child-care workers/teachers. They must be members for at least six months before they can serve with the children. This is for the volunteers' good, giving them time to get settled into the church body. It is also for the good of the children. We want to know our teachers before they spend time in child care with the children. Every child-care candidate is required to fill out a childcare application form, attend a child-care workshop and under-go a background screening. In the nursery/classroom, everyone keeps to the child protection policy, including important elements such as no teacher will be alone with the children at any time. The child protection policy was created under the supervision of the elders.

Resources at Home

We know that they are the primary spiritual caregivers of their children. We realize that parents have far more time at home with their children than we will ever have with them at church. But there's a lot we can do to support them as they teach at home. We try to support parents by teaching them well in their own classes and by the preaching of God's Word. We offer them book lists and hold book fairs of great books to use with their children. We pray for them by use of our members' directory. We provide take-home sheets and online resources that go with the curriculum we teach in the children's classes.

Teaching Them Well at Church

The Children's ministry team takes the elders' teaching recommendations and puts them into practice. They seek out good curriculum and good teachers to bring these biblical truths to life in ways that are understandable, enjoyable, and memorable. One elder, in particular, oversees children's ministry and helps them as they carry out the elders' recommendations. He also is there to help with difficult situations that arise with parents and children. He cares for the children's ministry team and ensures they are being spiritually well-fed, themselves. He keeps the other elders abreast of what is going on in children's ministry and seeks their advice on any matters as needed.

Supporting Teachers

Teachers teach in oversized teams which include more teachers than are needed to teach at a time. This allows us to put more experienced and less experienced teachers together. It also allows for someone to serve as a teacher, but not be "chained" every single Sunday to teach. This provides for vacation time, illness, and an opportunity to attend classes/worship services. It goes a long way to prevent burnout. We also provide teachers with opportunities to be mentored, to be observed, to observe someone else teaching their class, and workshops to improve their teaching skills. Hall monitors and deacons are on hand every Sunday to help teachers with any last-minute needs that arise or with escorting children to the bathroom.

Caring Well for Our Volunteers

About a third of our church is involved in childcare of babies or in teaching children. Since the elders want to make sure teachers are well-fed, they have set limits on how frequently teachers can teach. This is especially true for any teaching for children (as well as child care for babies) that takes place during the worship services. What happens if we have a consistent problem with filling teaching/child care slots with volunteers, given the elders' limits? First, the issue is brought to the attention of the congregation. Then, if the pattern persists, and enough new volunteers cannot be found, the elders choose to shut down particular classes. These will stay unavailable until a time when we have enough volunteers to fill those slots in a sustainable way. The elders give childcare/teaching provided during worship services as the top priority to fill. Childcare during the services may make a big difference in helping some parents learn from God's Word, and therefore, giving them better spiritual food to feed their whole family. They are willing to make up for a consistent shortfall in volunteers by closing other childcare offerings. A few years ago, they shut down Sunday School classes for a year when our volunteer numbers were too low as a way to ensure enough teachers/childcare workers during the worship service times. When the volunteer numbers came back up to a sustainable level, Sunday School was added back, grade by grade.

The Path to Gathering Together at Capitol Hill Baptist Church

Why the Elders Care to Create a Path
The elders hope that all children, 4th grade and up (ages 10+), will be a part of all the worship services.

For children under that age, they have provided options for children to gradually be a part of the worship services. This "ramp-up" approach helps children become familiar with gathering together with the congregation but is mindful that developmentally the whole service (especially the hour-long sermons) might be too much for some.

Many Roads Lead to the Same Place: All Preparing to Gather in a Way Most Appropriate

While the elders have set age limits that are the guide rails along what they think is a good path to gathering together, there are almost as many variations as there are parents in terms of how to get there.

Here are some of the variations the parents of these younger children choose:

What Families Do on Sunday Mornings

What Parents Choose to Do with Children Ages 0-5

| (MAY) ATTEND SUNDAY SCHOOL *AND* OUT OF CHURCH THE WHOLE SERVICE | OR | (MAY) ATTEND SUNDAY SCHOOL *AND* IN CHURCH UP UNTIL SERMON THEN GO TO CLASS | OR | (MAY) ATTEND SUNDAY SCHOOL *AND* IN CHURCH THE WHOLE SERVICE |

What Parents Choose to Do with Children, K-3rd Grade

| (MAY) ATTEND SUNDAY SCHOOL *AND* IN CHURCH UP UNTIL SERMON THEN GO TO CLASS | In addition to the regular worship hall, we provide a nursing moms' room with audio feed, and 2 rooms with video feed for families with noisy/wiggly/slightly sick kids to still take part in the service, but in an area more conducive for their needs. | (MAY) ATTEND SUNDAY SCHOOL *AND* IN CHURCH THE WHOLE SERVICE |

What Families Do on Sunday Evenings

As mentioned previously, our evening service includes a shorter meditation on Scripture as well as lots of sharing from the congregation and prayer. A great chance for the kids to hear about God's work in the lives of the church. This service is easier for kids to attend through the whole service, even the sermon, so we "shave off a year" of the out-of-service time, including the 3rd graders (8-year-olds) in the whole service.

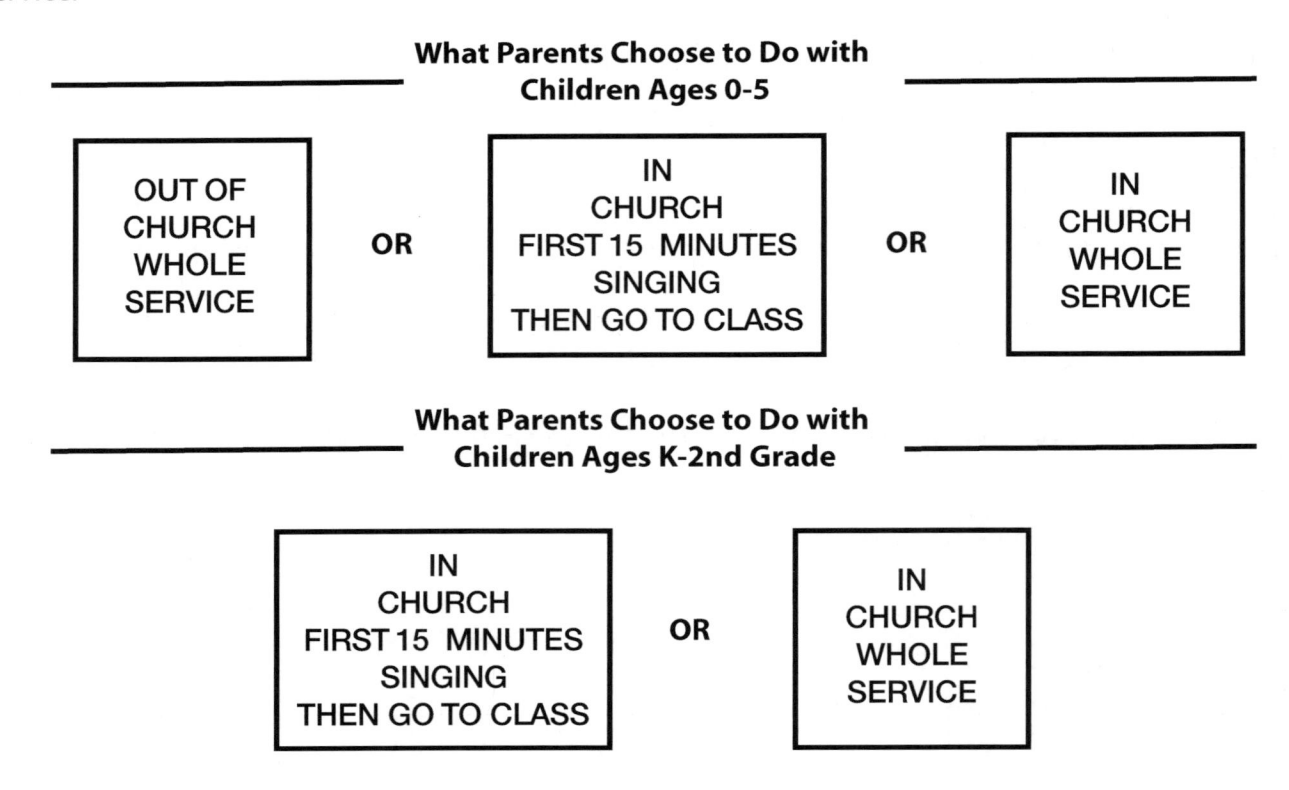

What Parents Choose to Do with Children Ages 0-5

| OUT OF CHURCH WHOLE SERVICE | OR | IN CHURCH FIRST 15 MINUTES SINGING THEN GO TO CLASS | OR | IN CHURCH WHOLE SERVICE |

What Parents Choose to Do with Children Ages K-2nd Grade

| IN CHURCH FIRST 15 MINUTES SINGING THEN GO TO CLASS | OR | IN CHURCH WHOLE SERVICE |

Preparing to Gather Together by What Families Do at Home

Our church has a sermon card that lets the congregation know what passage will be preached on. Some families read the passage together ahead of time, preparing their hearts for the pastor's sermon on Sunday.

Many take home and use the worship bulletins (especially the songs) to sing together at home.

We provide resources on our bookstall, in our church library, pastor give aways, and a huge, once a year book sale to provide our parents with resources to use at home with their children. (If you want a peek at what we offer in our book sale, the 40+ page booklist in available on the praisefactory.org website as well as on the CHBC website.)

THE PATH TO GATHERING TOGETHER AT CAPITOL HILL BAPTIST CHURCH

Preparing to Gather Together through Elements of Classroom Time

There are a number of ways we prepare our younger children in their classroom time to gather together with the whole congregation. The idea is to use elements of the regulative principle of worship in the classroom to prepare the children to gather more meaningfully with the church in the worship service. The Praise Factory curriculum, which I write for our church (available for free through praisefactory.org) is created with this very purpose in mind. On the next two pages, I'll describe how the regulative principle and use features of the Praise Factory curriculum as examples of how you can add these elements into whatever curriculum you use.

Praise Factory Curriculum: Mindful of the Regulative Principle

WHAT and WHY?
- Praise Factory curriculum seeks to help children to love God, live for Him, and worship Him with God's people.
- The regulative principle is a biblical summary of how God wants to be worshipped.
- Praise Factory incorporates the five elements of this principle into each lesson.
- This is to aid the worship of God during class time; and, to prepare the children to take part meaningfully in their church's worship services, where this principle is fully in use.

READ the BIBLE

PRAISE FACTORY RESOURCES
- Every Praise Factory Bible Truth is taken back to its biblical roots with a Bible passage.
- A kid-friendly explanation of the passage and any special theological terms is included.
- Every lesson also includes a Bible verse game with review questions as a fun way to encourage memorization, while also providing a simple inductive study of the passage.

PREPARING FOR A MORE MEANINGFUL WORSHIP SERVICE
- Bible reading in church sometimes includes concepts that children don't understand.
- Taking time to learn and explain these Bible passages and concepts in class can help children better engage with the Bible readings and preaching in the worship service.

PREACH the BIBLE

PRAISE FACTORY RESOURCES
- A story sermon presents each Bible Truth in the context of redemptive history.
- Some stories have a short span of only a single Bible story. Others include larger chunks of redemptive history (sometimes even the whole story from start to finish!).
- Each story is introduced with a listening question.
- The gospel is always included.

PREPARING FOR A MORE MEANINGFUL WORSHIP SERVICE
- The preaching of God's Word is central to your church's worship service. It can also be the most difficult part for kids to understand.
- The story sermon format provides a little dress rehearsal for listening to the preaching of God's Word in church.
- The biblical and theological content of the story sermons can prepare children to better understand concepts the pastor uses when preaching.
- The listening question helps children learn to listen with a purpose, just as adults do when God's Word is preached in the worship service.

THE PATH TO GATHERING TOGETHER AT CAPITOL HILL BAPTIST CHURCH

PRAY the BIBLE

PRAISE FACTORY RESOURCES
- Every Bible Truth is turned into an ACTS prayer (Adoration, Confession, Thanksgiving, and Supplication).
- This prayer format helps the children see how each Bible Truth points us to: praise God; confess our sins to Him; thank Him for what He's done through Jesus; and, ask Him to do great things in this world and in us, for His glory and for our good.

PREPARING FOR A MORE MEANINGFUL WORSHIP SERVICE
- These prayers familiarize the children with these same ACTS elements of prayer that they will hear in church.
- The practice of looking for ACTS in Scripture deepens children's understanding of God and hones their ability to glean truth from His Word, themselves.
- Hopefully these prayers will also become the children's own prayers that God uses in their hearts and lives, that they might be His people, the church's next generation of members and leaders.

SING the BIBLE

PRAISE FACTORY RESOURCES
- Praise Factory curriculum is filled with music. Music is one of the most powerful, long-lasting, memory tools God has given us... and it is so enjoyable at the same time!
- Each Praise Factory curriculum has a theme song.
- Every unit has a theological summary song.
- Every Bible passage is set to music.
- Hymns are included with important theological words and concepts explained.
- Even the classroom rules and other regular classroom elements are set to music.

PREPARING FOR A MORE MEANINGFUL WORSHIP SERVICE
- Music is an important element of every worship service, but sometimes the songs we sing in church include words or theological concepts children do not understand.
- Introducing Bible verse songs and hymns, and explaining their meaning in class can help children participate more meaningfully in church when the congregation sings, or Scripture is read.

SEE the BIBLE

PRAISE FACTORY RESOURCES
- "Seeing the Bible," in the classic, regulative principle sense, is speaking of the sacraments of baptism and Lord's Supper--the two "visual aids" Jesus gave the church to remember His work done for them and in them.
- Praise Factory curriculum definitely does NOT include these sacraments as activities. But, each curriculum DOES include a unit on the church with specific teaching on baptism and the Lord's Supper.
- In addition to this, the curriculum uses very careful language that holds out the gospel and provides a clear picture of how God's people live and worship, but without pressuring a decision or assuming conversion.

PREPARING FOR A MORE MEANINGFUL WORSHIP SERVICE
- Direct teaching on baptism and the Lord's Supper in class helps children understand these sacraments when they occur in the church services.
- Careful language about conversion and discipleship helps clarify what God requires of any of us before we can be baptized or partake in the Lord's Supper. This is especially important for sake of our children's souls and the purity of the Church. False conversion helps no one and has harmed many.

THE PATH TO GATHERING TOGETHER AT CAPITOL HILL BAPTIST CHURCH

The elders have chosen to stagger class offerings to create the up-ramp for gathering together:

SUNDAY SCHOOL HOUR
- ages 0-2 childcare (no teaching)
- ages 2-3: Hide 'n' Seek Kids (Praise Factory 1 "Theology" Bible truths)
- ages 4-preschool 5: Deep Down Detectives (Praise Factory 2 "Theology" Bible truths)
- K5-4th grade (5-10-year-olds): Gospel Project (Old Testament/New Testament Overview)
- 5th-6th grade (11-12-year-olds): Seeking Wisdom (Inductive BIble Study)
- 7th-12th grade (13-18-year-olds): Youth Core Seminars (Variety of topics for growing as a Christian.)

"Ramp-up" Notes for Sunday School:
1. Child care/Bible teaching does not interfere with worship service, so it is offered for all ages.
2. In Praise Factory classes, the children learn songs and prayers that will help them better gather together with the whole church. The stories used are more like story sermons, helping them prepare for more in-depth preaching in the worship service.

SUNDAY MORNING WORSHIP (The Main Preaching Worship Service):
- ages 0-2 childcare (no teaching)
- ages 2 childcare (no teaching)
- ages 3: HIde 'n' Seek Kids, pt. 2 (Praise Factory 1 "theology" Bible truths)
- ages 4-preschool 5: Deep Down Detectives, pt. 2 (Praise Factory 2 "theology" Bible truths)
- K5-3rd grade (5-9-year-olds): participate in worship service and are dismissed before the sermon for a separate teaching time. Praise Factory Investigators (Praise Factory 3 "theology" Bible truths)
- ages 4th grade and up (10+ year-olds): in the service the entire time

"Ramp-up" Notes for Sunday Morning Worship Service:
1. Two-year-olds just have playtime. One teaching time during Sunday School is plenty for these kids.
2. Three-year-olds, four and five-year-olds continue with Praise Factory curriculum that we have stretched over the Sunday School/Worship Hour and stuck play times in between, so both
3. Sunday School kids and those who only come to church will get teaching.
4. Worship bulletins are provided to help the K5-7th graders learn more during this service.
5. Younger elementary school comes in for the first part of the worship service (first 35 minutes) to gather together with the congregation.
6. In Praise Factory classes, the children learn songs and prayers that will help them better gather together with the whole church. The stories used are more like story sermons, helping them prepare for more in-depth preaching in the worship service.
7. Teachers and parents look for signs of readiness for kids to stay in the service and encourage this.

SUNDAY EVENING WORSHIP/WHOLE CHURCH PRAYER MEETING
- ages 0-preschool 5: childcare/Bible classes for the ENTIRE SERVICE
- ages K5-8: participate in singing time of the worship service and are dismissed for a separate teaching time. Great Commission Club (Missions)
- ages 3rd grade and up (10+ year olds): in the service the entire time.

"Ramp-up" Notes for Sunday Evening Worship Service:
1. Younger elementary school comes in for the first part of the worship service (first 15 minutes) to gather together with the congregation.
2. Because this service has a shorter preaching time; and, the sharing/praying content is more accessible to younger children, we lower the age limit on this class by another year down to 2nd grade (from the 3rd grade age limit for Praise Factory which takes place during the morning sermon).

Made in the USA
Columbia, SC
29 August 2024